A VOICE IN THE CITY

WORSHIP FOR URBAN PEOPLE

PETER HOBSON

CPAS
Church Pastoral Aid Society
Tachbrook Park, Warwick CV34 6NG

Scripture Union
130 City Road, London EC1V 2NJ

OTHER BOOKS IN THIS SERIES

The Well-Church Book by John Finney is a readable guide to mission audit.

Series editor Eddie Neale

Designed by Tony Cantale Graphics
Illustrations by Neil Pinchbeck

This book is sponsored by the Church Pastoral Aid Society, Athena Drive, Tachbrook Park, Warwick CV34 6NG. CPAS is a mission agency which exists to strengthen churches to evangelise, teach and pastor people of all ages. It seeks through people and resources to stimulate evangelism, equip and train leaders, advise about ministry and make grants for mission and training.

First published 1993
ISBN 0 86201 584 7

British Library Cataloging-in-Publication Data.
A catalogue record for this book is available from the British Library.

Printed in England by Ebenezer Baylis and Son Ltd, The Trinity Press, Worcester and London.

CONTENTS

PREFACE

A Voice in the City is about making worship within and from the culture in which a church is set. In Britain we live within a number of different sub-cultures. This book discusses the basic ingredients of Christian worship and considers the implications. How much should worship reflect the language and idioms and experience of the locality? How much should the music be the kind of music which is enjoyed by the congregation every day?

Peter Hobson writes from experience of the inner city of Manchester, although he now lives and works in a comparable area of Hackney, London. He has a proper concern for the kind of worship that is inclusive, and which holds together people from different sub-cultures. That is, he is truly 'catholic' in his approach. But he is deeply concerned that the hurts and oppression experienced in his part of the inner city should be reflected in the style of worship in the local church.

The principles about worship outlined here are applicable to every area. Even a church whose congregation listens mainly to Radio 3 and 4 could learn a good deal about rooted worship from this book. It is written with passion and from pain, in an attempt to relate what happens in the local church to the life which is experienced around it.

This is the second in a series of books published by Scripture Union and The Church Pastoral Aid Society which are intended to be practical handbooks for those who live and work in the urban priority areas of our country. Books designed for urban priority areas are rare. This is a venture of faith to provide practical resources for churches on the front line of mission.

Eddie Neale

Chapter 1

WHAT'S IT ALL ABOUT?

Seven out of ten people in Britain live in urban areas. Although that proportion is slowly declining, as people move out of the cities in search of 'a better life', still many Christians live and worship in urban areas. Yet the way we worship has largely been based on the patterns and assumptions handed down from a more rural age – or else has been developed by people who are principally suburban dwellers. This book is meant to do something to help shift that balance, for the sake of those of us whose lives are spent in inner-city and other less 'desirable' urban areas.

A snatch from Jeremiah chapter 29, verse 7 sums up what this book is about – 'for the good of the cities.' Jeremiah is writing to God's people taken as captives to Babylonia, about 597 BC. There were some around who were saying that this captivity was only a temporary thing – that very soon God would act to restore the nation of Israel and return the captives to their own land. So the temptation was to stick with the habits and customs of Israel and, above all, to have nothing to do with those wicked people who had taken them captive.

But God's word to them, through Jeremiah, was rather different. He told them that their captivity, far from being temporary, would last a lifetime and beyond. Ultimately God would, indeed, call them home. But for the moment their home was in Babylon. And their task was to get involved in the society where they found themselves. To marry and settle down. To work for its prosperity. And above all, to pray for it. If they wanted to work and pray for themselves, then they must work and pray 'for the good of the cities' where they were.

That is also the background to this book. Many of us find ourselves – by accident or choice – as city dwellers. As Christians we are also therefore 'urban worshippers'. How should we worship? It is my firm belief that we should not retreat into some form of 'Christian ghetto', but that instead we are called to follow the advice of Jeremiah – and work and pray for the good of the city in which we live. This book is about how we can do that better.

It's not a book about the whole range of things that will spring to your mind when the word 'worship' is used. And it will not begin to cover everything that goes on in the life of the city or the churches within it. To do either would take far more space than I've been allowed and I'd have to be far more of an expert than I'd dare pretend! What it *is* meant to be is not a book *about* the inner-city, but a book *for*

the inner-city. It is intended to help ordinary Christians living there to think a little bit more about their worship and so, I hope, to worship a little bit better.

Who wrote it?

So who am I to try and tackle this task? I'm an Anglican clergyman who has served all his ministry in the inner-city – 15 years of it, to date. Until recently all of it in one fairly limited area in two parishes in inner-Manchester, and now in East London. They've all been multi-racial and shared in most, if not all, of the things that usually go to make up what people call 'inner-urban decay' – as well as the many things that have made living and working here, for me, a rewarding and enriching experience that has become a total part of my life. At the same time I've developed an interest in how other people worship, both elsewhere in the Church of England, and Anglicanism overseas, and also in other churches about me. So what I write must be judged against that background. You may well be in a rather different situation – but I hope there'll still be points of contact.

Who's it for?

This book is written with some very particular people in mind. It's for Christians in ordinary inner-city or urban-area churches, who want to worship God better! Ideally then it's for people in a position to help that happen – not particularly vicars and ministers (who may anyway be excused for thinking they don't need 'yet another book' on worship!) – but for church elders, worship leaders ... or just anyone who comes to church and is willing to think a little more about what goes on and how to improve on it. And the test of success will be whether it helps real churches make real progress in their worship of a very Real God!

How to use it

A word about the book itself. In each chapter you'll find a number of 'Think spots', each one reminding you of some questions that have been raised by what's just gone before. If you can stop and think about those as you go it will help you consider what I'm saying in the light of your own situation.

If you're in the lucky position of being part of a recognised group of people leading worship in a church then you'll get even more from the book if you can agree to read it together and talk about it as you go. Maybe you could read a chapter or so then come together to discuss the questions raised. You might even like to keep a notebook and jot down the thoughts that occur to you at each point, to use as a reminder when you next meet with one another.

But however you do it, it's the applying of the book to *your* situation that matters. No outsider knows your congregation or your church in the way that you do, and the ideas which look great on paper can prove a disaster when applied to a different situation. On the other hand, sometimes another way of looking at things can help you see new possibilities in a situation you thought you could do nothing about. And if new possibilities lead to new ways of worshipping that bring people closer to God – then it's all been worth it.

Chapter 2

LIFE IN THE CITY

'Do you believe in a God who can change the course of events on earth?'
'No, just the ordinary one.'

From *Inner-City God* by Geoffrey Ahern and Grace Davie, Hodder and Stoughton 1987

What's all the fuss about?

That quote comes from a survey of the attitudes of white working-class people in Tower Hamlets to God and the church. It's easy to laugh at – but it shows the way many ordinary people feel about life in the city. They are trapped in a situation that can't be changed. And God – if he is there at all – is no more able to alter things than anyone else!

To people who don't live in the city it can be hard to appreciate what all the fuss is about. I grew up in a medium-sized town, with the hills always in sight beyond the roof-tops. On half-term holidays in the summer my Mum would sometimes pile us into the car and we'd drive up there for a picnic by a stream. Beautiful. Idyllic even. But not what we can easily do for our children now we live in a city!

There are as many experiences of city life as there are cities, or even people living in them. Neighbours living side by side may have totally different experiences of life in their street. And you will have your own experiences of city life which are particular to you, the area you live in, your 'history'.

What I'd like to do in the next few pages, therefore, is not try to 'sum up' everything in life, but instead take you through an imaginary 'day in the life' of a typical inner-city area. It will be open to the charge that it concentrates on the negative things; for many of us there is also a definite 'up-side' to inner-city life. But it would be foolish to pretend that the bad things aren't there. Or that they don't affect a lot of people, both in church and out of it. We need to face these fair and square if we are to move on to look for God at work in the city – and to respond to him in our worship.

A day in the life...

The day gets under way slowly. Those who are working on the early shifts may be up and out anytime from 5am onwards. Others stay in, sleeping off the effects of last night until noon and later. Mums are up (most of them) getting the kids ready for school and from 8.30 onwards the streets fill up with children being taken – or taking themselves – to school. Some come on their own, as young as five or six. And a good number get themselves ready, and wander in late. The teachers don't like it, but they're used to it. It's hard to get up on time if Mum's been out on the streets half the night.

As the morning wears on more people appear wandering off to the shops. A queue forms outside the post office – too many people wanting benefit, too few staff to pay them. The post office noticeboard is covered with postcards advertising second-hand prams, gas fires, builders services and puppies. And the wall around it is like most walls in the area – covered with graffiti. Like the litter in the streets, however fast you may try to clear it up, it just appears again as if by magic.

The chip shops open for the dinner-time customers: a mixture of the junior mechanic with a multiple order for the rest of the lads, and others working in or passing through the area today. Local residents are fewer in number than at the evening opening hours. Mostly you only go for one chippy meal in a day and that's when there's more of you at home. The discarded papers blow about the streets, together with drinks cans and crisp packets and the odd discarded porno magazine. All blow indiscriminately into small front gardens or down alleyways. No one thinks to take their rubbish home – whether they're visitors or locals. The street is just one vast litter-bin.

Dogs also patrol the streets, singly or in groups. Mostly they avoid people – although the people may find it harder to avoid the mess they leave behind. Sometimes a vicious snarling indicates a dog's dispute. Or a flurry of barking tells of another car being chased. Less often someone gets chased or bitten. It's seldom reported. Who to? What could they do?

As the afternoon wears on it gets to school home-time. Another procession of push-chairs and uncles meanders to the school gates. Many older children take their younger brothers and sisters home with them, crossing main roads as they go. They all call into the corner shop or at the ice-cream van for some sweets, if they have any coppers to spare. Between now and midnight the streets are never free of children, all ages, playing out, kicking a ball about, chatting on corners, or plotting dark deeds round corners. They may well have homes to go to – but apart from the afternoon 'soaps' there's little to keep them in. And for more than a few, Mum or whoever isn't back until gone six anyway.

As dusk falls life begins for some. Darkness is the invitation to all sorts of new adventures. The day may have been spent mainly asleep, or in aimless wandering. Perhaps for some it was the time to do a bit of robbing to finance a drug habit. For these people the dark alleys and corners are a haven to do the deal and collect your 'stuff'. The discarded needles and syringes may be found the next day – perhaps by an inquisitive child. If they're lucky they'll avoid the sharp, and possibly infected, ends. In certain well defined areas the girls take to the streets in search of 'customers'. Sometimes it's boys too. In these parts pedestrians should beware of looking at cars and drivers of slowing down near walkers. Either action may be mistaken by someone as indicating a search for business.

The pub trade is slow until mid-evening, but picks up later on. Chucking-out time may lead to a drunken argument or two, but the streets usually soon quieten again. At weekends it may take longer, and the arguments may assume noisy proportions at midnight and later. A scream may split the night air – but it's not at all clear whether it's a genuine cry for help or part of an overheated dispute. Honest citizens (and others) ponder whether to call the police.

Finally, in the small hours, the clubbers start returning home. Some by taxis, if luck has treated them kindly that night. Others by late buses, or on foot. As the last of these straggle home, the first of the early workers are up and about again. And the cycle repeats itself, again and again, without apparent hope of change or alteration, for all the government intiatives and church reports. This is life on the streets of the city. This is home for so many of the people of our land.

Audrey and Margaret were elderly sisters, living in a tower block built on the same site where years before they lived in an old back-to-back terraced house. Twice in one month the young man in the flat above them came in at 2am, turned on the stereo (loud!), ran himself a bath, and promptly fell asleep. Twice they were woken up, first by the stereo and then by the trickle of water through the ceiling, soon turning into a gush, until one of them could run upstairs and wake the upstairs tenant up to turn it off. When they complained to the Housing Office they were told: 'These people have to live somewhere. There's nothing we can do.' What has Christian faith to say to Audrey and Margaret? What to the upstairs tenant?

Our response?

Of course it's not all as bad as that may sound. There are also many positive things about living in the city. The friendships. The vitality. The tremendous breadth of life that is often present in the community. The lack of pretence that so often accompanies suburban living. I've lived almost all my adult life in the city and wouldn't for one moment want to run city life down. But having said that, I also wouldn't want to romanticise it. Life *is* hard for many people. The environment *is* unfriendly. People's lives *are* often in a mess. As far as the world is concerned it does feel as if we live in a 'forgotten' zone, where 'out of sight' is 'out of mind'.

And the church is part of this life. Yet at the same time it exists to be a sign of hope to it. A sign that there is a better life. But not one that just involves getting rich or getting out. A way of life that connects our city life with that of the city of God. God's life can shine into our kingdom of despair with rays of the kingdom of heaven. Yet how can the everyday life of the urban church look like this to those both inside and outside its walls? That, for the most part, is the theme of the rest of this book.

THINK SPOT

1 How much of "A day in the life ..." do you recognise in your own experience of city living? What would you add to it?

2 In recent years there have been a number of initiatives in city areas from governments, local councils and churches (for example the Anglican 'Church Urban Fund' and the Government Inner-Cities programmes). How much difference do you think they have made to the situation?

'On the other side'?

In all major cities there are boundaries. Sometimes they're obvious, other times more invisible. Often they're moving! But they exist and are real. They're the boundaries between the places people like to live and the places they don't. Maybe it's a main road that makes the division, or a railway line or a river. Maybe it's just down to the type of houses that are there. But you can tell where it is by the way people choose to move house if they get the chance. And by the prices they have to pay!

Where I lived in Old Trafford there's a long road called Ayres Road that's a wonderful example of 'boundaries'.

- At one end, across another road, are some large tower blocks. When they were built they were filled with the people who used to live in the old terraced houses they replaced. Now, as those people have grown older and thinned out, they tend increasingly to be for 'problem tenants', so creating a 'problem area'. People don't like to stay there long if they can help it.
- Moving down the road you come to some larger houses, which are either shops beneath and flats above, or else privately rented and in multiple occupation.
- Down the side streets are rows of terraced houses, two-up, two-down with the front doors opening onto the streets. Good first-time buys for some, a long-term home for others.
- As you pass further down the main road, suddenly front gardens appear, even the odd tree. The houses get bigger and more of them are owner-occupied. And, of course, the prices go up!
- Then Ayres Road crosses another street with large four and five-bedroomed semi-detached 'desirable residences', with substantial gardens: homes the average university lecturer might not be ashamed of!
- Finally we come to the railway line. On the other side is the part of Old Trafford that likes to call itself 'Firswood'; a post-war development of smaller modern private houses. Many moved out there as part of a deliberate process of bettering themselves. Their attitudes to the part they have left behind can sometimes be revealing!

That's where I lived. In other areas it will be different, and the boundary may be the edge of a large council estate, perhaps even on the edge of a city. But it will still be a boundary. People will know where it is, and which side of it they live on. And which side they want to live on!

And there's a very important

question relating to these 'boundaries'. Which side of them do the people who worship at your church come from? And which side of them are the people whom your church wants to reach out to – and so to join your worship? These sorts of questions are explored some more in John Finney's book in this series, *The Well-Church Book*. But their implications for worship are obvious.

The sort of worship that suits people who live in tower blocks may be different from what suits those who live in semi's. If the congregation are mostly of the second sort then how easy is it for them to plan worship that helps newcomers of the first sort? We'll look at this sort of question again in chapter eight.

City living

All the above is a description of city life as I have experienced it. There are, of course, other types of inner city area and other aspects of life that could have been touched on. But the overwhelming impression will be the same. City life has its many good aspects, of course. But the depressing reality is that a solid backdrop to them all is deprivation. Deprivation that can be analysed and split off into different headings, but they all add up to the same thing. 'They' don't care about 'us'.

There's economic deprivation – that's poverty and homelessness. Social deprivation – that's family breakdown and lack of amenities. Environmental deprivation – that's dirt, squalor and grotty surroundings. Political deprivation – that is, in most inner city areas there's often little at stake politically in helping change things, since your party is either guaranteed seats or hasn't a hope of getting them.

And, all too often, there's spiritual deprivation as well. For alongside the picture painted above is another story. The story of the church in the city. The story of evils ignored and opportunities lost. Of responses to need that were either too late or totally misplaced. Like the nineteenth century Church of England response to the discovery that the masses imported into the newly expanded cities of the industrial revolution for cheap labour were not going to church. So what did they do? They passed an Act of Parliament and built more churches for them to go to. But never stopped to ask why the working man stayed away from a church that was run, financed and

THINK SPOT

1 Where are the 'invisible boundaries' in your area? What marks out the differences either side of them? Where is your church building in relation to them? Where do your congregation come from?

2 Why do people move from one side of a boundary to another? What does that say about how they view the people they may have 'left behind'?

3 How well, in your experience, do people 'on the better side' understand what it's like to live 'on the other side'?

... never stopped to ask why the working man stayed away.

attended by the people who built the very mills that exploited him! To summarise the conclusions of Bishop David Sheppard in his classic book, *Built as a City*, it is not that the church has lost the urban working classes. It never had them in the first place.

And in the twentieth century the story has continued. Since the end of the First World War church attendance across the country has plummetted, and the old social ties that still bound people to the institution of the church, if not to regular or committed attendance, have one by one been snapped. We now live in a truly post-Christian society. Churches that could boast of queues for seating, at least at the major festivals, now struggle on with twenty or thirty people in a place built to seat over thirty times that number. During these years the city itself has also been changing. People have been moving out to more suburban areas in large numbers, as both census figures and personal experiences bear witness. The inner-city has become increasingly a community of the 'left behind', of those with neither the power nor the money to choose to move. Increasingly, not only the people at the top, but also many of those in the middle have used the city as a work-place, but have retreated to the town or countryside for recreation and leisure.

In the late-twentieth century we have begun to see a second industrial revolution. The old industries, built around the harnessing of natural resources for power, have suffered severe, often final decline. The marvels of the micro-chip have replaced them. And the increasing cost of transport has caused many to reconsider living so far from where they work. City life changes once again. But once again, who can doubt that those with power and money will be pushing for change, and making sure they are the ones who benefit from it. So complexes like Liverpool and London's Docklands, or Manchester's Salford Quays spring up on the decayed sites of former key industrial sites like docks and canals. Homes are built for the wealthy. The leisure industry rushes in to provide playgrounds for those with money to buy it. But once again the ordinary local city-dweller looks on, largely excluded. Largely denied hope.

It has been said that the Bible begins in a garden and ends in a city. So city life can't be all bad – nor is it! Of course there is more to it than the bad things listed or described above. But we ought to begin by looking these squarely in the eye and acknowledging them. Only then are we free to move on to point to the good, or to highlight what the church is doing to speak from within the situation, rather than bewail it from the outside.

THINK SPOT

1 Think about city life as you experience it. List the top five things you appreciate about life in your area. How would you write a prayer to thank God for these for use next Sunday morning?

2 Now list your top five complaints. Write some short prayers for use in Sunday worship, ending with the same phrase and response, sharing those concerns with God.

The rest of this book

So far, this book has touched on a number of aspects of city life; in later chapters we'll go on to look at how the city church handles its worship, in the light of these. But first we'll begin, in chapter three, by looking a little more closely at what city churches are like from the inside, especially as far as their worship is concerned. We'll also think a bit about what we mean by 'worship', in any case.

In following chapters we'll pick out various strands of this backdrop we've painted, and think about worship in the city against that background. For example, chapter four is called 'Worship on the other side' and will think about what worship means in an area of physical deprivation and poverty.

Chapter five is about ourselves and the way we bring our hurts and painful experiences to God, rather than burying them or pretending they're not there.

Chapter six will think some more about the importance of the way we feel in our worship and also about the place of different types of music in city worship.

Chapter seven is about language; about what we say to God, and how we say it in a way that city people can best use.

Chapter eight tackles the important topic of the multi-racial nature of many inner cities, and about what that has to say to our worship, both from the point of view of other non-Western Christian cultures and looking at the impact made by people of other faiths as well.

Chapter nine will consider the age-range of people our worship aims to cater for, and will try to point out some ways the family of the church can respond to some of the good things city dwellers have in their family lives without making them feel too bad about the other things.

Finally chapter ten will look at how our worship relates to the wider community about us, and how they see and relate to us.

Then, for those with real stamina, there's an epilogue to suggest ways you might take it all forward!

Chapter 3

FAITH IN THE CITY

'The liturgy...must give authentic expression to the common life in Christ of the people of God present at each particular gathering, in whatever generation and in whatever country and culture.'

(Report of the 1988 Lambeth Conference)

Worship in the city?

What is typical city worship? Is there such a thing? Some would deny it exists – surely as God is the same everywhere, so to worship him is the same wherever we go? But the quote above, from the 1988 gathering of Anglican bishops from across the world, suggests another way of looking at it – even if it is written in conference-ese. God may be the same everywhere – but we are different. Wherever the cultures we live in differ, so also our worship of God must differ as well.

But of course people differ in outlook and temperament as well, wherever they live and worship. City people, like people everywhere, are divided between evangelical and liberal, quiet and noisy, musical and tone-deaf – and so on. Churches vary in their outlook and traditions, so there isn't anything that could quite be described as *typical*. But if the last chapter described some common factors of inner-city life, so there may well be common factors of city worship. So let's take a look at what might be happening some local city churches this Sunday, through the eyes of three people who might be attending.

Thank God it's Sunday!

Sonia attends a Pentecostal church, or more accurately one from the tradition known as the Holiness movement. Like most of the congregation she is black, but born and brought up in Britain. Her parents, who came to England from Jamaica in the 1950s, used to be Anglicans, but have belonged to this church since shortly after they arrived in this country and were told, when they turned up for Sunday worship as usual, that 'your church is down the road'.

The morning begins with 'Sunday School', but not, as most British churches know it, just for the children. Sonia is a class leader and so teaches a group of juniors, including two of her own children, but a good number of the adult congregation also turn up for their own classes in different parts of the building. After Sunday School everyone gathers in the church for worship, which gets under way as soon as enough are there to begin, but people will be arriving (and, to some extent, leaving) throughout the service. Sonia is part of the 'junior choir' (the 'senior choir' is largely limited to older members who were born 'back home' and value a slightly different style of music), and she joins with others in leading the loud and joyful music, with hand-clapping and harmonising. Sometimes a member of the congregation steps up to lead the rest in a song of their choice, and later on Sonia, who has a powerful voice, is asked to sing a solo.

A little later the minister invites the congregation to pray – and most do so, out loud, and together. Over the noise various voices are heard, and gradually the minister's prayer (he has a microphone!) takes over and all listen and join in with a resounding 'Amen' – or more likely, a 'Praise the Lord'. The sermon follows; Sonia gathers that some people think 45 minutes to an hour is a bit long, but she knows that the Word of the Lord is to be heard and treasured – and dull the preaching most certainly is not! There is passion, there is conviction, people are exhorted and challenged – and the congregation responds vocally throughout. Today, as a climax to the service, is the monthly 'breaking of the bread'. A real loaf of bread is used and non-alcoholic wine. The service ends sometime in the early afternoon and Sonia gathers her children to her and they make their way home for a late-afternoon main meal.

Chris prefers high-church Anglican worship. He comes from a local family of several generations standing, but the congregation is a mixture of black and white, locals and incomers who prefer this style of worship to that on offer at churches nearer home. As Chris and his fellow-worshippers gather, the church bells are rung. The service follows a home-printed text, but the priest adds a number of words and gestures, some of which are familiar to Chris, others relating to a particular theme for the day. The whole feel is of colour and light, with several banners and candles. At various points Chris makes the sign of the cross which helps him remember who he is worshipping and why. As he listens to a brief, seven-minute homily he recalls that the preacher at his friend Sonia's church is much more expansive and wonders whether, when it comes to sermons, it's better to be starved or bloated! It's Chris's turn to lead the prayers (he's one of a small group who do so), and he does so by following a set form, with a few topical additions of his own. The main focus is the eucharist, as it is called. The bread (wafers actually) and wine (the real thing) are treated as very important, and Chris is part of the small procession that brings them forward at the right time. Their importance is reflected in the way they are prayed over and handled after prayer.The service lasts perhaps one-and-a-half hours and once it is over Chris returns home quickly.

Our final worshipper is Jean, who is a member of an Evangelical Free Church, in the Baptist tradition. Although originally brought up in the area, Jean and her family, along with most of those 'running' the church, now live some distance away, having moved out some years ago at a time when council clearance policies changed the face of the community. The congregation is again multi-racial, but most black faces are overseas students from a nearby university.

Jean plays the oboe and is a member of a small orchestra, who lead the singing of modern choruses, mixed in with more traditional hymns. Jean's husband, Phil, is 'taking worship' this morning (a role not open to women in Jean's church) and he opens with an extempore prayer for the service. This is followed later by a longer, but similar, prayer for the church, the community, overseas missions and the preacher – who is their part-time pastor. His sermon, which is long but illustrated with overhead slides at points, is the main focus of the service. As he concludes Jean slips out before the final hymn to make the tea and coffee which most worshippers stay on for, along with a friendly chat about the week.

Many and varied

Each of these three churches is typical of just one style of worship you might find in a city, and of course there are many others besides. Sonia, Chris and Jean may know each other quite well – and there again they may not. They all seek to worship the same God, in churches set in the same community – but in quite different ways! There are, of course, at least as many varieties of patterns of worship in cities as elsewhere in the country. Indeed once you add in the presence of other faiths – which it is not within the scope of this book to explore – you begin to see that in at least some inner-city areas there is far more real worship going on than in many more suburban or rural settings. One of our long-standing local teachers, himself not a believer, once commented to me that he'd never worked in such a religious community.

Faith in the City

In 1985 the report *Faith in the City* was published by the Church of England, the end-product of two years of work by the Archbishop of Canterbury's Special Commission on Urban Priority Areas. Early in 1990 came *Living Faith in the City*, a briefer follow-up report on progress in the intervening five years. Together these might be said to represent the Urban Priority Area 'Bible', and they address more or less the whole range of issues facing Christians (and others) living in the city. *Faith in the City* therefore includes a section on worship which comes up with comments such as these:

- worship must emerge out of and reflect local cultures.
- it will be more informal and flexible in its use of urban language, vocabulary, style and content.
- it will promote a greater *involvement* of the congregations in worship.
- it will reflect a concern for things to be more concrete and tangible rather than abstract and theoretical.
- people should be encouraged to come and go.
- worship is important as a means of evangelism.
- worship will recognise harsh realities but put them in a new light.
- running through it all must be a recognition of 'the importance of the ordinary'.
- formal liturgies must be complemented by more informal and spontaneous acts of worship and witness.

To sum it all up, *Faith in the City* says that the church should aim to 'be present in celebration, confession, compassion and judgement'.

In an attempt to discover how far the

A church warden in a northern parish admitted to the new vicar and his wife that he could neither read nor write, but that he very much wanted to do so. He began to take lessons from them and set himself the goal of reading a lesson at the Carol Service. By Christmas he was up at the lectern to do the reading. It was slow; it was halting – and doubtless for some listeners it was hard to follow. But it was a triumphant expression of his place before God in that church. True worship was taking place!

people on the ground shared these views, some of them were 'tested out' on both clergy and lay people in a survey of attitudes to worship amongst Anglicans in inner-city Manchester in 1986. The full results are included in an appendix at the end of this book, but some of the more revealing results are given here. For example when it came to the importance of 'speaking clearly', nearly two lay people out of three strongly agreed 'those leading worship should pay special attention to pronunciation and clarity of diction' (although one in three clergy thought so!) But nearly half of those asked also thought it 'very important that ordinary members of Urban Priority Area churches are encouraged to join in leading worship.' There seems to be some conflict here in what is needed in those who lead worship. This point will be taken up again in chapter seven.

And when it came to 'the practice of coming and going during a service', less than three in ten clergy could agree that this was 'not to be discouraged' and only one in ten lay people agreed with them! What *Faith in the City* encouraged was obviously not entirely what Manchester Anglicans thought!

Living Faith in the City (the follow-up to *Faith in the City*)notes two main changes in city life in the late eighties. The first, particular to the Church of England, is the work carried out by its Liturgical Commission resulting in a report *Patterns of Worship*, which sets out to tackle worship for urban parishes. The second, perhaps more general, result is what that report calls 'a fresh impetus on the part of many clergy and congregations to explore forms of worship arising from their own experience'. It goes on to quote as a goal some words of the German theologian, Jurgen Moltmann: 'It is possible that out of a church *for* the people there could come a church *of* the people. In place of a religious ceremony for the people each Sunday there can be a feast of the congregation.'

So what is worship?

So far we've been talking about 'worship' as though we all knew and agreed what it meant. But of course we don't – as the examples at the beginning of this chapter show.

Can we get any nearer to an agreement about what worship is? Does the person who says 'I can worship God just as well in my garden' have anything in common with the neighbour who much prefers the full elaborate ritual of a High Mass? And does worship in an inner-city area have

THINK SPOT

1 Discuss with your group what you think of the views of *Faith in the City* on worship as outlined on page 17. Perhaps you could 'score' each point from 1–5 ('Strongly agree' through to 'Strongly disagree') and then compare notes on what you felt and why.

2 Should the church warden in the story above have been allowed to do the reading? Why – or why not?

any different features – or emphases – compared with worship elsewhere?

The Bible has quite a lot to say about worship – not surprisingly – and many, many books have been written on the subject. But as this isn't a book about the little details of worship or the finer points of liturgy I don't propose to go too far into histories of why we do things the way we do. Instead, at the risk of over-simplifying an important subject, I want to suggest a very basic approach to what we are trying to do in worship.

The aim of worship

When looking for a biblical definition of worship we can start in several different places. But one of the most important for me has always been Paul's description in Romans 12 of what he calls 'true worship'.

'Offer yourselves as a living sacrifice to God, dedicated to his service and pleasing to him. This is the true worship that you should offer.'

(Romans 12:1)

If this is so, it means that to worship is to try to make ourselves into such a 'living sacrifice'. And so our worship is as much about the lives we lead as the actual things we say and do in church.

If we go on to ask what are the most important things that God requires of the lives we lead, we could turn to some words of Jesus. When asked

which commandment was the greatest, he replied :

'The most important one is this. "Love the Lord your God with all your heart, with all your soul, with all your mind and with all your strength." The second most important commandment is this: "Love your neighbour as you love yourself".'

(Mark 12:29-31)

There are two other important biblical pictures of worship we should note as well. The first comes when Jesus is replying to a Samaritan woman who had asked him the classic poser of the time, about where the true God is to be worshipped. He also speaks of 'true worship' and says that

'God is Spirit, and only by the power of his Spirit can people worship him as he really is.'

(John 4:24)

And in the vision of heavenly worship in Revelation 4–7 we see with John the twenty-four elders who 'fall down before the one who sits on the throne, and worship him who lives for ever and ever.' A little later we see an enormous crowd of people 'from every race, tribe, nation and language' who 'stand before God's throne and serve him day and night in his temple.'

In both of these pictures we can see that worship is first and foremost not something that is centred on us and our needs, desires, or preferences, but on God. It is about who he is, and what he is doing in the world – and beyond it!

Putting all this together means that:

- worship is not just what we do in church on a Sunday, but part of our everyday lives.
- worship is first of all about our response to God.
- worship is secondly about our response to our neighbour.
- worship is only thirdly about ourselves.

Or, in the words of the simple but effective children's chorus:

'J-O-Y, J-O-Y surely that must mean Jesus first, Yourself last, and Others in between...'

Methods of worship

It's all very well to say that worship is about all of life. But we still do, most of us, aim to gather together week by week. And unless we genuinely feel we can 'reinvent the wheel' each time we do so, there obviously there has to be a framework of things to say (or sing) and a structure to work within. And that framework must stand the test of being able to let us do the things listed above as being important in what worship is.

Traditions vary as to the place they give to 'liturgy', by which most people mean 'set words'. In fact the word 'liturgy' comes from a Greek word *leitourgos* which originally meant 'the performance of public duties', and it's a similar word, which originally meant 'hired labour' or 'service', that Paul uses in Romans 12:1 for 'worship'. So a word originally meaning 'serving others' came to mean 'serving God' and so to be used for 'worship'. Perhaps we keep elements of that when we talk still of a 'worship service'.

Anglicanism began, of course, on the principle of 'authorised services', in which using the specified words was paramount, and using any other words was an offence punishable by law. The non-conformist tradition has long reacted against this, and the early Puritans were indeed most suspicious of any attempts to prescribe exact words to be used in worship. Roman Catholic worship has always combined a respect for the 'magic of words' in themselves (especially, until not so long ago, in Latin!) with an equal recognition of the importance of the actions used, at least by the priest, at the Mass.

We have moved some way from all that today, when on the one hand many non-Anglican churches have their own printed 'service books', and on the other the 1988 Lambeth Conference could recognise that authorised liturgical forms 'provide but a part of the actual events of the liturgy' and go on to look for 'a far greater freedom, which has its own marks of the Spirit'. And Catholic worship has similarly opened up, with the virtual abandonment of Latin in favour of local languages, and moves in many places towards far greater recognition of the involvement of the whole congregation, lay and ordained.

Ingredients of worship

My skills in cooking are a standing joke in my family, and our sons love to relate how the first time Daddy made a cake Mummy choked on it! Perhaps that's not quite fair: whilst never aspiring to Cordon Bleu I turn my hand to the cooker whenever necessary, and I know enough to realise that a cookery book can be invaluable. Mostly they offer you first of all a list of ingredients followed by instructions on how to mix it all together and cook it. The whole picture can actually be applied to worship as well, and just as in cooking the many possible ingredients fall into a few broad types, so the many types of ingredient that go to make up 'a service of worship' can be classed into four main areas.

Things that help us to listen to God

- this will naturally include the 'Ministry of the Word', that is the reading of Scripture and some form of explanation of it (which will include but needn't be limited to just the traditional sermon!).
- silences are good here too.
- for some churches 'listening to God' will mean expecting him to speak through members of the congregation, through the use of charismatic gifts.

Things that help us respond to God

- this can be done through led prayers or music.
- silence can again be good.
- the chance for personal response may mean a vocal contribution, eg in open prayer or the choice of a song or hymn.

- this can include the chance for people to discuss between themselves and assess what they have heard.

Things that help us to talk to God

- prayer is, of course, often described as 'talking to God' although there are many other forms of prayer. But 'intercessions' certainly qualify under this heading.
- 'talking to God' may include anything that offers words that 'sum up' how we feel about ourselves and about those close to us, and about things that concern us or other people.

Things that help us relate to one another

- The Peace is, for Anglicans, a recently rediscovered way of doing this, which can work well or be appallingly embarrassing – depending how it's done!
- this may also include the use of small groups to, for example, discuss a sermon or to consider topics for prayer, or even as prayer groups in themselves.

All these things will be different in different traditions of worship. You can and should work out for yourself what they will mean in your church. And the rest of this book is intended to help you work out what, in particular, they will mean for the sort of church that is to be found in the city.

But as in the kitchen, the proof of the pudding is in the eating! Sometimes you can have all the ingredients right and still the end result is tasteless and uninspiring.

THINK SPOT

1 Either get an order of service, or make notes on how a typical service in your church goes. Then go through it and decide how the various items used fit into the four groups of ingredients mentioned above. Do you have any ingredients that don't fit these headings?
2 Are there ways you'd have liked to change the overall balance for the better?
3 Are there things that make it easier or harder to 'light the oven'?

We may do the mixing but it is God who lights the oven! And, as Jesus told the Samaritan woman, unless we worship in Spirit and truth we do not worship at all!

A definition of worship

So we can end this chapter by attempting to put all this together and come up with a 'working definition' of worship. You can then use this to 'test' whatever else I say or you think as we go along. The key question will be: 'Does this activity/line of thought help towards worship, as here defined,or doesn't it?' Here it is:

Worship consists of bringing my world to God and of finding God in my world.

THINK SPOT

What do you think of this definition of worship? What would the average person in your church on Sunday think of it? How would you test what happened in your church last Sunday morning against it?

Chapter 4

WORSHIP 'ON THE OTHER SIDE'

'If you ain't got nothing, nobody won't come to give you anything.'

(from *Inner-City God*)

From this part onwards on we'll be looking at the particular things that might make city worship different from worship anywhere else. I'd better say again at this stage that there's no such thing as a 'typical inner-city church'. So there may be churches who don't recognise themselves in some of what follows, but on the other hand a lot of it may well apply to churches in areas that are by no means city – inner or outer!

The quote at the top of this page is from someone who knows only too well that they live 'on the other side' of one of those 'invisible boundaries' we looked at in chapter two. Someone who feels in their bones that whatever good may be going on in the world, they'll never see anything of it! Inner-city churches are almost always 'on the other side' of these boundaries. How do they begin to help local people discover that something good *is* going on on their side – that God can be discovered and worshipped, in Jesus?

Spot the church

The first thing about churches 'on the other side' is that, like much else about them, their buildings are often not their strongest point! It's become almost a

truism in some circles that 'the church isn't the building, it's the people.' And of course, like most truisms, that's 100% correct. The New Testament never ever talks of the church as a physical building – although, of course, in several places the church is likened to a building, most notably in 1 Peter 2, where we are called the 'living stones' and Jesus himself is likened to the keystone of an arch ('the most important stone of all').

But, also like most truisms, it can become so accepted without question that the 'other side of the story' gets forgotten. And in this case, the 'other side' is the buildings of bricks and mortar which all church congregations inhabit! Theologically they may well not be anything like as important as the people they house – but try telling that to the death-watch beetle, the dry-rot spores, or the Historic Buildings Preservers. And when the frozen worshipper half-way back in some church is desperately trying to let their spiritual temperature rise above the close-to-zero degrees Celsius that is around them it may not help to be exhorted that 'we can worship God anywhere'. (Especially if it's said by a clergy-person swaddled in several layers of liturgical garments!)

The blindingly obvious fact is that the buildings we use to worship in *do* affect the sort of worship we can offer to God, either for better, or for worse. And we could do with some creative thinking about how they affect us so that we can make the most of whatever the good Lord and previous generations of his people have given us.

A barn or a mistake?

Of course there are, thankfully in increasing numbers, church buildings that do positively help their congregations in their worship and witness. But, partly for historical reasons, city churches do tend to suffer more than most from their buildings. The problem sort tend to fall into three categories. First there's the vast barn, then the tin tabernacle, and finally the sixties' mistake. Let's consider each in turn.

The vast barn

This is typically a large Victorian edifice, built to the greater glory of the benefactors – although the early decades of this century saw some comparable vast buildings as well. Many cities saw their major growth periods in the nineteenth century commercial boom that put Britain at the top of the world league for such vital commodities as cotton, civilisation, and cricket. And they are circled by churches built in those years. My former home city of Manchester is just one such. The churches were built on the money made out of the textile trade (and sometimes the slave trade as well, although such churches would normally be somewhat older). They might seat up to 1,000 worshippers and, in the generosity of the benefactors, many of the seats you wouldn't even have had to pay to occupy! They were built on what was then the edge of the city, with green fields beckoning beyond, and the middle-class worshippers rode to church in their carriages, whilst their servants, perhaps after being sent off to early morning service, rushed back to prepare the Sunday lunch their employers would return to.

But the generation that built them has long since passed on, as have their children and theirs besides. Passed on either to whatever reward or otherwise awaits them in the next life, or to the undoubted reward of a modern, centrally-heated and luxurious abode in today's desirable out-of-city locations. What they have left is a series of monuments to an age that has passed by. But unfortunately they mostly haven't left the cash to hold those monuments in repair. Nor do their spiritual successors necessarily have the desire to worship in monuments or to spend most of their energies as their caretakers, whatever they or others might ideally like to be the case from the point of view of nostalgia or history.

So the 'vast barn' type of church building presents its occupants with a number of problems. The first is how to keep it in sufficient repair to be usable with any degree of safety, let alone comfort. The second is how to use it for worship of a type which is almost certainly rather different from that for which it was originally designed. And a third is how to plan for the future of that church when so much time and energy can be taken up with the up-keep of the said building.

Some congregations have managed to make the best of such churches and reorganise the interior away from the 'serried ranks' that they were towards a more participatory and welcoming sort of style. But combining that with vast areas of vertical space can lead to the worst of both worlds, whereas suspended ceilings or even community rooms can be vastly expensive. Others have managed a more radical approach and decided to demolish and rebuild from scratch. This, too, is very expensive, but has the merit of producing a result more in line with the needs of the church today. But if this course is opted for it's worth planning for flexibility, remembering that we don't want to leave our successors in the next century feeling as anguished about what we pass down to them as we have done about some Victorian buildings.

The tin tabernacle

Other church buildings were more modest, but their very modesty, combined with years of neglect, has brought them to the stage where only major overhaul can make them usable with comfort once more. The classic 'tin tab' was indeed made not of tin, but of corrugated iron, and gave adequate shelter to its faithful congregation of thirty or forty when it was built. Perhaps God has been at work, and the congregation has indeed now grown closer to the 100 mark. But they are left with a church building that is to their needs what post-war pre-fab housing is to a modern luxury home.

The solution is probably similar. Either major rehabilitation or, if vision and finance permit, a total rebuild. Finance can vary of course depending on circumstance. If the church concerned is in an area where land value is high, and has a postage-stamp of land to sell they can probably rebuild their church and still have a balance to put into ethical investement for the future. But for most churches money will be a major factor in what can be achieved. For what it's worth, our own experience is that finance can follow vision better than vision follows finance! See below for more about this.

The modern mistake

The final type of problem church is different in nature, and stands as a salutory warning to those who prefer radical solutions. For the radical sixties made some radical mistakes – and trusting some of the architects and builders of their generation was one. Some purpose-built churches less than twenty-five years old have already been abandoned as little better than inverted sieves, the repair of whose roofs would cost far more than the whole building cost when it was new. It comes as little comfort to know that many local authorities have fared no better, and are nowadays busy demolishing system-built flats whilst still paying off the interest on the original building costs!

Such buildings may be salvageable, at cost. Certainly modern building techniques have improved, and the use of a qualified architect – who knows about church buildings (not all do!) – is a must. But they warn us, even more vivdly than the previous two examples, that like people all buildings have a natural life-span. They are conceived, then built; they are put to good use; they need tender loving care to keep them in good health; even so they take ill from time to time and need to be made better; and eventually the kindest thing may be to allow them a merciful release at the kind hands of the bulldozer. No building lasts for ever, just as no person lives for ever.

But the difference is, of course, that when buildings die they die. With people it is different. For Jesus came to offer us eternal life. And that is why, at the end of the day, we have to say that, however much buildings have to be thought about, the real work of churches is about people, not buildings. So it's to the needs of people that we return.

Worship in buildings

But not to forget buildings. As we've noted above, they do affect our worship and it's time to think about how, and what we should do about that. They can affect worship either for the better or for the worse.

For the better

- the very way our buildings look can echo aspects of the character of God. For example churches with masses of space overhead (what architects call 'the vertical dimension') can help 'draw our thoughts upwards' to God.
- some beautiful things in them can

focus our feelings as well as our thoughts on God. Stained glass does this for many people, but the same thing can also be done with, for example, banners. The quality and arrangement of furnishings and lighting can also help us appreciate the beauty of holiness through the holiness of beauty.

● the way churches are built tends to back up a particular understanding of what the church is all about. For example rows of pews from front to back speaks of a congregation whose main job is to sit and 'take' whatever is delivered to them by the minister. Seating that enables eye-contact between worshippers underlines our togetherness in worship, and movable seats or empty spaces can allow room for people to meet each other after the service.

● the very age of some buildings can give positive associations, reminding us of the continuity of worship 'down the ages', especially if there's a feeling of 'stones saturated with prayer'. (Even if we're not sure what that means theologically, it's a common feeing emotionally.)

For the worse

● all the above points can be not so helpful as well as helpful! For example as well as highlighting some aspects of the character of God, the way buildings are can obscure others; beautiful objects can distract our thoughts away from God rather than lead them to him – and not everyone shares the same ideas of beauty anyway. And as the earlier example shows, buildings can hinder as well as help particular understandings of the church from being realised in worship.

In addition there are the following points, particularly relevant in many city churches:

● standards of comfort that suited one generation may be unacceptable to another. (Is there a cinema or town hall in your town or city left unaltered for even ten years, let alone 50, 100 or longer?)

● smaller congregations may 'rattle around' in over-large buildings.

● the sheer cost of looking after a large church may swallow up all the money and energies that a congregation has, leaving nothing over for beginning to look at adapting it to changing needs, let alone deciding what the church is there for in the first place!

THINK SPOT

1 What do you think your church building and its furnishings are 'saying' about God?

2 Is that the main thing we want to say about God ? (Consider this firstly from the point of view of those who worship regularly in it, and secondly those who come only occasionally, or perhaps see it only from the outside.) If it is, well and good – but how do we bring in other important things? If it isn't, then can we do anything about it?

3 How are we using the spaces in our building? Go round it space by space and ask what you are doing and what you could do with that space. Think laterally!

Can we afford it?

Many churches have problems with money. It's not necessarily that the people aren't generous. In fact a Gallup Survey taken alongside *Faith in the City* showed that city congregations were often far more generous than those elsewhere. But because congregations tend to be smaller, because often buildings-related costs are higher, and because there's far less of a 'fringe membership' to appeal to for fund-raising, the finances can get a bit tight!

But we need to ask ourselves some important questions about money. It tends to be that the sin of people in 'comfortable Britain' is to be obsessed by money itself, whereas the sin of people in 'uncomfortable Britain' is not always to spend what they have wisely. In the light of what Jesus said, for example, to the rich fool in Luke 12, I'd think the latter far less serious than the former.

When it comes to spending money, then, splashing out on things to do with worship can seem to be a bit of a luxury. A new set of song books may seem a lower priority than fixing the leak in the roof. And too much money spent on the inside of a building may make some people feel uneasy anyway. But from the point of view of this book, spending money on helping us to worship is money spent just about as well as it might be. Because it's money spent on helping us 'bring our world to God, and find God in our world'. Which is what we're supposed to be all about.

So whatever the financial pressures in your church, you could do worse than sit down with a blank sheet of paper and list all the things that you'd like to provide to help your worship work better. Here's a list of some things you might check out just for starters:

- carpetting an area of the church that is at present cold floor, to give that 'warmer' more 'homely' feel.
- creating an area for a creche, so that worship for those with children is more of a positive experience, less of an ordeal (more of this in chapter nine).
- looking at your furnishings – table (altar?), lectern, chairs, cloths etc. Are they a bit tatty and in need of touching up, or replacement?
- what about a lick of paint on the walls?
- speaking of song books, have you got enough of them? Do they include enough of the songs and hymns you want to sing? Do you have Bibles for everyone who comes? And are all these books in good condition, or do they need repairing or replacing?

When you've listed all these items, and others that will occur to you as you go along, go through them putting a price to each, as best you can. Then a priority on each. This may be best done through a discussion in some leadership group in your church. Then go to whoever organises your church's money and ask how you can begin to find the money to do some, at least, of these things, in order of priority. A tall order? Not if you believe that the setting for our worship counts as much as the content of it.

THINK SPOT

How could the above exercise be carried out in your church? What would be the good things about doing it? What (who?) are the likely obstacles? Should you do it this year, next year, some time or never?

Local is best?

There's one final thing about worship 'on the other side' that we need to consider. It concerns the question over whether we should aim for worship which is truly local or worship which is 'the best'. For some people these two are one and the same thing. They would say that if worship is 'bringing our world to God' then we can only do it properly in our language and using things that are real in our everyday life. Others, however, would see worship and local life as almost complete opposites, especially in the cities. In an area of deprivation, they argue, we should aim to lift people beyond what they have, to offer them a glimpse of something better, and higher. Something more worthy of God.

The quotation from the Lambeth Conference report at the beginning of chapter three also looks at this tension from another angle. The Lambeth bishops said that whilst worship must have something in common across all churches and cultures, it's also important that it properly reflects the culture and way of life of the actual people worshipping there.

Of course, not everybody sees it that way. In the survey carried out in Manchester diocese clergy and laity were asked their views on the following two statements:

Those leading worship should pay especial attention to pronounciation and clarity of diction

and

It is very important that ordinary members of Urban Priority Area churches are encouraged to participate in leading worship

Although 42% of lay people 'strongly agreed' with statement two, 63% also strongly agreed with statement one. In other words although a good number of lay worshippers thought it important that people like them help lead worship, two out of three felt strongly that this was only if they could learn to speak properly first. Interestingly, the clergy took a different line, and only 34% strongly agreed with statement one whilst 55% did with statement two.

Also, when asked to comment on a further statement that: 'the language of worship should be adapted to suit the local culture', only 8% of laity and 22% of clergy strongly agreed. This does seem to point up a tension between different views about 'ordinary people' leading in church – at least amongst Manchester's inner-city Anglicans! There is still felt by many to be a 'proper way' to do things, and to

I remember once discussing worship with a group of clergy, some of whom who were astounded that, for example, ordinary people were encouraged to pray aloud in services. 'They wouldn't get it right' or 'that's not decently and in order' seemed to be the assumptions behind the questioning. I was saved on that occasion by the intervention of another clergyman who offered the unanswerable defence, 'But the people meet with God'. And that, if true, should be an end to all complaint!

diverge from that way is perhaps seen as a little dangerous.

Of course a problem with aiming to make everything local is that if you try to worship God only using what you have to hand, then you can end up with a seriously limited picture of who God is and how we can understand him. So, for example, although Jesus' stories about farmers and fishermen may not be as easily grasped in a modern urban culture as in first century Palestine, or even in more rural twentieth century Britain, we don't drop them from our Bibles. We work on making them real.

But, on the other hand, the problem of looking for 'excellence' outside the local culture is that it will tend to run down local people. It can also make wrong value judgments about what is 'the best' or the 'most godly'. It's by no means obvious to me that Handel's 'Messiah' is of more value than a school nativity play with a black Joseph and Asian angels, or that BBC English is better understood than the local accent.

We need, as well, to remember that there may be more than one 'local culture'. In many cities there are a rich variety of cultures, and it's possible this may be reflected in the church as well. One church I know of, with a number of overseas students also in the congregation, celebrated the Chinese New Year, followed by an African afternoon and a Caribbean evening all in rapid succession. And churches with any Asian Christians in them will have still more variety of resources to draw on. There's more about this in chapter eight.

The short answer, then, is that excellence in worship is an OK thing to aim at. But there are proper differences of opinion about what is 'excellent' in a given church. And, of course, worship that we see as excellent, God may see quite otherwise. Remember the story of the Pharisee and the tax collector (Luke 18). And do you recall God's words through the prophet Amos about the sort of worship that ignores wider issues of justice and righteousness? He said, 'I hate your religious festivals.

THINK SPOT

1 If some typical local residents wandered into your services by accident (it does happen!), in what ways would they feel 'at home'? In what ways 'out of their depth'?

2 What is there in your local culture that could be brought more into your worship?

Stop your noisy songs; I do not want to listen...' (Amos 5). But that's another matter again.

Church and politics

To talk about inner-city areas is to talk politics. Perhaps already you've been annoyed – or heartened! – by some of the references in this book to what you'd call political issues. When *Faith in the City* was published, one response was to condemn it as yet another example of a current trend for the church to get too involved in politics, one anonymous Cabinet minister even condemning it as 'thoroughly Marxist'! Interestingly enough the follow-up report *Living Faith in the City* was far better received. But it's hardly surprising if the concerns of politics and religion overlap sometimes. After all, each in its own way is concerned with how to serve the people and meet their needs.

Certainly, city churches cannot help noticing the deprivation about them. After all most, if not all, of their congregations live with it day by day. And, as we've noted, this has its own political dimension. In the words of the Brazilian Archbishop Helder Camara: 'When I give the poor bread they call me a saint. When I ask why the poor have no bread they call me a Communist.' Politics and the church is a major issue in its own right – too major to do anything like justice to in a book concerned mainly with worship.

But in the light of the quotation from Amos above, it is not only possible, but even essential that we spend at least a little time asking how politics relate to worship?

Sadly, churches often tend to polarise between those that see community and political involvement as the very essence of the faith and those that see these things as a betrayal of the true gospel. Worshipping in the first sort of church you will be regularly exhorted to pray for the unemployed and the victims of military dictatorships, although perhaps less often told what is specifically Christian about the particular line taken on those issues. Worshipping in the second sort you could probably be forgiven for thinking that all the church is about is snatching souls out of a wicked world for a glorified sing-song in heaven.

These are extremes, of course. There is a middle way, and it's a very important one to discover. Because, as we noted earlier, the gospel is about love for God and love for neighbour. It's both about how as individuals we find our way to peace with God and about how we live our lives alongside one another in this world. So our worship should reflect this.

Worship that takes seriously the local politics and community will leave room in the prayers for local concerns. Occasionally room will be found, preferably at some time in Sunday worship, for more in-depth exploration of a Christian approach to such issues. If the congregation is fortunate enough to include anyone active in local politics it will include prayers for them – but also for their colleagues and opponents. If there are no such people in a congregation we should ask why. Is it perhaps that those of strong political views are not welcome in church? In a church that takes its community seriously the calling to be involved with and so love our neighbours through the means of local politics will be part of the church's message. The 'notices' will include items of general public interest, and encourage members to support them. And preaching will begin as often as not with the items that make the headlines in the news or form the basis of discussion on the doorsteps.

THINK SPOT

1 What are the sort of issues that have concerned your local community in the past year? Which are recurrent? Which were 'one-offs'? What response was there to them in the worship of your church?

2 Can you remember a recent sermon which helped you understand a current political issue better? If so, can you explain to someone else what it said to you?

Summing it up

Those of us who worship 'on the other side' are trying to bring to God a different sort of life to that which most churches' traditions are used to coping with. We need to ask some basic questions of our inherited traditions. Questions based on our understanding of what worship is meant to be about – 'bringing our world to God; finding God in our world'. We need to be prepared to follow the answers wherever we judge the Lord to be leading us.

Chapter 5

WORSHIP OF THE WOUNDED

The minister had just announced the Confession and the congregation fell to their knees, eyes closed. It was just as well. For a voice rang out from the back, 'I confess my sins,' and into church came a middle-aged lady who had shed her coat to reveal underneath nothing but her underwear. She was a wounded worshipper!

All of us are wounded worshippers – although not all may express it in quite such unusual ways as the (true) case above! One picture of the church that is around today is that of an army, usually portrayed as 'on the march', or 'ready for battle'. And in such an army the stragglers or walking wounded are of little help, and so of little value. It's a popular picture, although one with surprisingly little Biblical justification (In the Bible, usually God fights for us, not we for him!)

But long ago Augustine described the church as more like a hospital, where we are all the patients, sick and in various stages of recovery. We may indeed all look to help one another in our progress to health, but it is Christ himself who is our doctor, nurse and ward orderly.

All this is true of worshippers in 'comfortable Britain' just as it is of worshippers in 'uncomfortable Britain'. But by the nature of city life there are many more people around in inner-city areas who are vulnerable, hurt and disturbed. What should be our attitude to them? How can our worship make room for them? How can we learn from them? – for many of them are indeed ourselves.

The hurts we suffer

There are various types of wounds or hurts, as I'll call them from now on (it's just that 'wounded' begins with same

letter as 'worship' and makes a better title!) that tend to affect people . Here are just a few.

Hurts from childhood

Things that happened to people long ago, perhaps in childhood or infancy, have got in the way of their proper emotional development. The extent of child abuse – both physical and sexual – is now known to be far greater than was previously recognised. Every victim is thereafter a hurt person – for the rest of their lives, or until that hurt is healed. These hurts can make it hard for us to trust people; they can make us hard to get close to; they can make us very angry people, which may or may not show on the surface; they can make us unforgiving – and unable to accept God's forgiveness for ourselves. But what these symptons have in common is that the solution is always where the hurt is – deep down inside us. And no amount of casual 'jollification' in worship will change that.

Hurt by poverty

Few people ever think they have 'enough'. But most people in this country know nothing of what it means to be really poor. Statistics on poverty are notoriously hard to interpret, subject to political manipulation, and usually several years out of date by the time they appear. But to give just a couple of examples: *Living Faith in the City* states that in 1986 5% of households had a gross weekly income of below £40 and 18% of households had £60 or less. House of Commons Social Security Committee figures show that in 1988 21.6% of households lived on less than half the average income – that's 11.8 million people, and compares with a 1979 figure of 9.4% of households (4.9 million people). It does seem that poverty is a real, and growing phenomenon in Britain. Of course poverty is a relative term, and few people in Britain face the extremes of starvation of many overseas. But even 'relative poverty' can be crippling – and there are plenty of families who have literally no money in the house, no bank account, no savings, and no food either for several days until the next Giro comes. Many of these have young mouths to feed as well. Such poverty dominates your horizons. Life becomes a constantly wearing search for enough for the next week. Such poverty is on the increase in Britain today – and urban areas are where a lot of it is to be found. Like most clergy in the inner-city, my week is punctuated by callers at the door asking for help. And whereas in times past it was often 50p for a bus fare (being translated as 'towards the booze'), nowadays it's far more likely to be a request for food or help in getting a bed or a cooker or other essentials of living. Although many such people have no time for the church – and the church often appears to have no time for them – sometimes they also are to be found seeking the Lord, and trying to worship, with their wounds.

Hurt by unemployment

As well as all the problems of poverty mentioned above, unemployment brings other hurts. In a society which tends to value us by 'what we do', to have no answer to the question 'What do you do?' can led to a deep loss of self-worth. Life can take on a timeless and meaningless quality. There is a younger generation growing up which has no stake in our society, a society which by settling for high levels of long-term unemployment has seemingly agreed that certain people will be deprived of the God-given opportunity of work. These people also come to worship, seeking reassurance and help in their need.

Hurt by prejudice

Another form of hurt that can only be partly understood by those who haven't experienced it is the hurts given by prejudice – especially racial prejudice. There'll be more on this in chapter eight, but for now we should note that most if not all black people in Britain have experienced racism, not just from the blatant few, but in more subtle forms from the oblivious many. It hurts to be told, 'Your church is down the road', as many first-generation West Indian Christians were, or even worse, 'Thank you for coming, but please don't come back. People wouldn't like it.' It hurts nowadays to be expected, as is too often the case, always to sit at the back, perhaps to hand out the books, but never to offer an opinion or take a lead. It hurts young people to be categorised in headlines as 'Black Youth Riot' – whoever saw a headline 'White Youth Riot'?

It hurts to be stereotyped as 'good at sport' but 'slow learners', as too many schools have tended to treat black pupils. And when all these types of hurt are brought to the experience of worship, alongside white sisters and brothers, it hurts all the more to be told: 'In this church we don't notice the colour of your skin. We are all the same really', when your whole experience in British society has been so very different!

Hurt by 'the system'

Then there are those who have just always got on the wrong side of 'the system'. Who perhaps were brought up in care; who perhaps have been left in unsuitable housing for too long and no one will listen or act; who perhaps have their parenting skills questioned by social workers where others are given the benefit of the doubt; who perhaps are arrested when others are simply 'warned off', or jailed when others get probation. All these things, and many others besides, are the common experience of a significant number of city people – and the backdrop to how they feel about 'authority' in general, including 'the church' and God.

Hurt by drugs

I've deliberately not added 'or drink' because, of course, alcohol is just another drug and so is already included! In some city areas drug abuse may not be a major problem, but in many others it is. Sometimes it's associated with prostitution. What sort of welcome can we give in our churches to those whose lives are damaged or destroyed in this way? What sort of images do they bring to the worship of God in the first place?

THINK SPOT

Which of the above sorts of hurts do you think affect people in your congregation? Are there other hurts that you would like to add?

Hurts of the mind

Finally, there's a group of people whose wounds are deep inside their minds: those with mental health problems, whether short-term or long-term, whether under treatment or simply never formally diagnosed. Current policy is placing more and more of such people 'in the community', which sadly often means with families who have no real help or support or, more commonly, in hostels which offer little more than bed and breakfast. These, also, will often be found seeking attention from the community of God's people, and deserve to be received with love and understanding.

Hurts in worship

If part of worship is 'finding God in our world', then it stands to reason that it includes finding him in the parts of our world that hurt. But, sad to say, a lot of what passes for worship leaves no room at all for our hurts even to be brought before God, let alone to be dealt with. In a bit we shall be looking at that second question of how we can make space in worship for God to deal with our hurts. For now let's look at the first matter – how do we allow them to be brought before him in the first place?

We can begin by noting that there is one concept of worship that seems to allow very little place for our feelings, whether of hurt or of joy. It is a form of worship where everything is tightly controlled, usually from 'the front'. A form of worship where everything that happens is known and planned in advance. Where the unexpected is not expected – and not made welcome if it occurs! In this idea of worship it can seem that the task of the worshipper is to 'set aside' everything about themselves at the church door, and join in a ritual where everyone is playing some sort of holy game. Especially we can be expected to 'set aside' the hurt bits of ourselves, that might make for unpleasant scenes. It is, I think, a peculiarly British sort of worship, and owes a lot to our Church of England heritage where the written service was everything, although it can equally happen in places with a supposedly 'free' tradition, but where in reality the unwritten liturgy is at least as controlled as a written one. But whether or not it is a good sort of worship for other areas, I don't myself think it is particularly helpful in city areas. People need to feel that there is space for them to come as they are. That they are allowed to be themselves before God in church as much as they are a few minutes earlier with their families and friends outside. Indeed that they might be even more themselves in church than before. But just how do we set about doing that? There's the difficulty.

Acknowledging hurts in worship

There are some obvious points in most services where this can come in. For example, most church services have a time of Confession, usually quite early on. But the problem here is that often Confession is starting too far down the road. Confession is what we do with things that we acknowledge as sins. But there are a lot of things deep down inside us which we either don't admit to as sin or, far more likely, that we call sin, but are really hurts caused by sins committed against us – like the sort of things we looked at above. And to encourage people to confess to things that aren't sin is as bad as not encouraging them to confess things that really are!

A period of quiet before Confession can be of real value to many in giving space to consider just how we *do* feel, before rushing into words, whether spoken for us by others, or a set prayer to join in with. Of course some people, with encouragement, might be able to make time to do this at home, or on their way to church – but for many others that is hopelessly idealistic. If we don't offer people space for reflection at church, some just won't get it at all!

Another obvious place to acknowledge hurts before God is in the prayers, or intercessions. There can be few churches which do not have a time when the sick and suffering are prayed for – often by name. Perhaps there's a chance for individuals within the congregation to add names out loud or pray at greater length for someone. In some cases names can be written down in advance in a book or handed to whoever's leading worship. There's room here for sensitive leading of the prayers so as to allow people to *include themselves* in those being prayed for. For example, rather than praying for 'the sick: Mrs Jones, Mr Smith and anyone else known to us' you can invite prayer for 'Mrs Jones, Mr Smith and all those here with particular difficulties or needs today'. And particular groups of people can be used as a focus for prayers on occasion – for example the unemployed, or the victims of crime.

> Andrea confessed in a small group that she had 'really let God down' when she swore at her brother who had been picking on her all day for her faith and punching her more and more painfully.
>
> The group told her she was right to feel angry at his behaviour and more right to react than to bottle it up and act 'meek and mild'.
>
> Who was right? How would you have advised her?

There are, however, other ways to allow the expression of hurts in worship. Music can have great value here, as we shall see more in the next chapter. There are many hymns and songs, both new and more traditional, that can unlock feelings that words alone would never touch. Some churches may be ready for times when a number of suitable songs are simply followed by silence or the opportunity for people to pray aloud about their own needs. Or for a minister to put words to the feelings that are deep in their hearts.

Of course worship can also be brash and insensitive to other's feelings. There are those whose taste in worship tends to songs or choruses full of statements about how good we feel, or of extravagant declarations of our love for Jesus. There is a place for such worship. But we need to be aware when we invite people to 'sing it as if you really mean it' that perhaps some of us don't, at that precise moment, mean it at all. Of course, the sorrow of some should not limit the praise and joy of others. But it works both ways. The joy of some should be sensitive to the deep hurts of others.

And hurts and joys can go side by side in the same person. It's not at all impossible to raise hands in exuberant praise and yet have in a corner of your heart a deep-seated pain over someone or something. Indeed it's surprising how often the two do go together.

Finally there is the power of the Word of God and of preaching. Although this is not primarily a book about preaching, we cannot talk about worship without including some reference to it. In cities especially it is important that a variety of the many ways of preaching are explored, but in all of them there must be scope for the Word of God – described in Hebrews 4:12 as 'alive and active, sharper than any double-edged sword' – to reach deep into people's hearts.

The good preacher has the ability – this is both practical and spiritual! – to touch people's needs and bring to the surface things that are otherwise buried deep. And having brought them to the surface, to point people to God as the one before whom they can express themselves.

THINK SPOT

1 Is your worship 'tightly controlled', or is there room for people's feelings of hurt and sorrow to be offered to God?

2 Supposing you had just been told that a member of your family had been seriously injured in a car crash? At what points in your service could you find a chance to bring that before God?

3 When you are worshipping with enthusiasm is there space for hurt people not to join in, without being made to feel spiritually incompetent? If not, can anything be done about this?

The healing ministry

If opportunities to bring our hurts to God are taken, and people begin to feel that feelings of hurt are allowed to be part of worship, then things will begin to come out. But once they have come out – what do we do with them? How can we deal with them, appropriately and helpfully for everyone?

Dealing with hurts can also be described, quite simply, as healing. The rediscovery of the healing ministry of the church is one of the more hopeful signs of our times, and nowhere is this more true than in the cities.

There are, of course, many ways that

ministry can be shown. One way is simply through the love that is present in a congregation and between people. This is something that worship cannot create, but it can foster it and give expression to it. If it is in order for one person to be in tears and for their neighbour to turn and comfort them, without anyone else batting an eyelid, then probably you've gone some way in this direction.

Another way is through a more formalised 'prayer for healing' ministry. In many churches this takes the form of an invitation, perhaps at particular services, perhaps regularly – for any who feel in need of prayer to come forward (or to some other part of the building) and then others will lay hands on them and pray for and with them. Some churches may also make use of anointing with oil, in line with long-standing tradition and the words of James 5:14. For some this will be 'sacramental oil', specially blessed; for others it will simply be 'from the bottle', but in each case the intention is to offer a further physical sign of healing, to accompany the prayer.

Those involved in the praying may be limited to just the minister(s), but it is better to extend involvement to a carefully selected group. Often it is best to have people praying in pairs, one male, one female, so as to ensure that there's always someone of the same sex as the person being prayed for. Perhaps sometimes threes might work as well – though we need to beware of an unseemly 'scrum' about people! And, of course, confidentiality is vital – so that anything that may be mentioned as a cause for prayer does not then become a matter for general discussion!

Such ministry is best backed up by a counselling ministry as well. Issues that arise in the context of prayer can be followed up afterwards, or later in the week. Some may require much prolonged counselling; others may need referral to those better qualified to help. But at least there has been opportunity for the hurt to be acknowledged before God, for the healing power of the gospel to be brought to bear on it, in the context of worship. In some churches only the minister is recognised as being competent to do this, whereas elsewhere there may be others who also fulfil this role. Even where there is no one formally assigned to counselling often you find someone quietly picking up the pieces behind the scenes. Such people need to be identified and encouraged. They can sometimes be helped by some simple training course. But counselling is a vital part of healing ministry, and someone who will just *listen* may be all that is needed at first.

Similarly, alongside this 'service centred' ministry can go a person-centred ministry, in the home or perhaps a suitable church office. Again traditions and practice will vary, but there is room for a wide range of approaches, from personal confession to God in the presence of a minister who can offer assurance of forgiveness, through counselling ministry as detailed above, to deliverance minstry, which focuses on the presence of spiritual oppression. This last can be the cause of some division, but it is my belief that, if we wish to be faithful to the ministry of Jesus and alert to the reality of the work of Satan in the city, we need to be open to the reality of this dimension of hurts and healing, in a matter-of-fact and unsensationalist way.

The 'wounded healer'

In case you've not come across it before, that's a phrase to describe the person who helps others whilst still needing help themselves. For some that's a contradiction in terms. 'How can he help others when he's not even got his own life sorted out?' people say. Which in a strange way echoes what some said of Jesus on the cross: 'He saved others, but he cannot save hmself' (Mark 15:31).

Others suggest that in fact it's those who accept their own need of healing who can most help other people. Certainly if we wait to offer help until we are ourselves perfectly well, we'll wait for ever.

THINK SPOT

1 If your church has any form of formal healing ministry, how is it developing? Or is it about right for your church and for what God wants to do among you?

2 Who do people tend to come to, to talk over their problems? What help are these people given in handling this counselling?

The proper expectation that church leaders ought to be people worthy of a measure of spiritual respect is not at all to be confused with the heresy that they should be above temptation or without problems. Paul himself, who was never slow to offer advice to those in need (and those who probably felt they weren't!), could write that 'we are able to help others...using the same help that we ourselves have received from God' (2 Corinthians 1:4).

So it may be that often the person best equipped to lead worship is the one who from their own experience knows some of the hurts shared by the congregation, and so can be more sensitive to how to handle things that touch upon those hurts. Also, when it comes to healing ministry, the minister may be as in need as any of the congregation and there should be scope for him or her to seek that help from amongst the congregation. But at the same time there should be no pressure that he or she 'ought' to seek help first. It may be that actually they are quite well adjusted at the time. Or that there is no one there whom they feel they can quite trust with their problems.

THINK SPOT

1 What sort of expectations do people have of those who stand 'up front' in your church? Are they fair ones?

2 'How can he help others when he's not even got his own life sorted out?' Can you decide when this is a fair question and when it isn't?

Summing it up

We do ourselves no favours if we carry on pretending that we are all 'beautiful people' offering well-crafted worship to God. It's not true anywhere – in 'comfortable Britain' or 'uncomfortable Britain'. But city people are perhaps better – certainly we ought to learn to be – at bringing to God that part of our world that hurts. After all, as Jesus said: 'People who are well do not need a doctor, but only those who are sick. I have not come to call respectable people to repent, but outcasts' (Luke 5:31-32). So we will learn to find him even in that part of our world that hurts the most – perhaps especially there!

Chapter 6

WORSHIP FROM THE HEART

City churches must 'be prepared to communicate through feeling rather than the mind, through non–verbal communication rather than verbal'.

(From *Faith in the City*)

What a mixture!

'I am fearfully and wonderfully made,' said the Psalmist, and he (or she!) was right. We human beings are an amazingly complex creation! One of the ways we sometimes simplify that complicated bundle of thoughts, feelings and ideas that is you or me is to divide ourselves up into different parts – for example body, mind and spirit, or perhaps head, heart and soul. This can be a helpful way of describing different aspects of ourselves – or it can be an excuse for ignoring some parts of ourselves, or keeping them firmly in their place!

Some people, we say, are 'all heart' whilst others are 'all head'. An army is reckoned to march on its stomach, and some people also seem to live for their food or other bodily needs! But the truth is that God made us not as lots of people rolled into one, but as one person with lots of different aspects, and life is lived best when we let each part of us have its proper place in the whole.

This is as true of our worship as anywhere else. It is possible to approach worship in different ways. For some people the real test is, 'Is it true?' or, 'Does it teach me something about God'. For others it may be, 'Will it make me feel good?' or, 'Will we meet with God?' It is important to remember that these needn't be opposites but can all be proper

questions to ask. Paul, writing to the Corinthian Christians, described his own feelings about speaking in tongues when he explained that: 'If I pray in this way, my spirit prays indeed, but my mind has no part in it.' He clearly saw this as a difficulty and went on to ask: 'What should I do then? I will pray with my spirit, but I will pray also with my mind' (1 Corinthians14:14–15).

The quotation at the head of this chapter reminds us of one of the things we said in chapter two about those of us who live in inner-city areas – that we may be more open than people elswhere to communicating through feelings as well as words. This is a good thing, but it does run against much of the trend of traditional worship which, being centred on *the Word*, has also gone on to be centred on *the words*. So how can our worship learn to welcome the non-verbal parts of us without losing out on the good things that words bring? That's what this chapter is going to explore.

Signs and symbols

In some Christian traditions signs and symbols are very important. Indeed it's generally regarded as only extremists who would now interpret the Second Commandment as meaning that churches should offer only bare white-washed walls to take your mind off the preacher's sermon or the length of the hymn! But the types of signs and symbols we are happy with and how we use them are very wide and varied.

Christians of the more 'Catholic' traditions have tended to be best at using such things. Their churches may be full of statues, paintings, wall-hangings and ornate crosses and they have richly decorated cloths and hangings, with changing liturgical colours throughout the year. More Protestant Christians have tended to avoid many of these things, in favour of decoratively scripted versions of the Ten Commandments or the Lord's Prayer and Creed, and scripture texts. I know of one Pentecostal church which has painted round the panels of its upper gallery sixty-six different pictures, one drawn from each book of the Bible, each with its accompanying reference. It certainly offers wide scope for increasing your biblical knowledge during any boring bits! Of late the charismatic movement has brought fresh influences, so it is now probably more usual than not for a church to have hanging somewhere a banner or two made by church members. Our own church was probably not unusual when we went through a period of making a fresh banner annually to coincide with the church motto for the year. Then, of course, there's stained glass – practically the hallmark of a church building! And although we often think of ancient or Victorian art in this context, there's a lot of good modern stained glass as well.

In some churches it's traditional for some or all of the people leading worship to wear distinctive robes or other clothing. One of the defences that is given for this practice is that it symbolises something about worship, in that it points out clearly the leaders,

and yet offers a degree of anonymity so their individual personalities don't get too much in the way. On the other hand some might feel that leaders ought not to be marked out so distinctively within the whole people of God, and that individual personalities that are going to get in the way of worship are hardly going to be stopped by as trivial a matter as the clothes they are wearing!

THINK SPOT

Make a list of the 'signs and symbols' used in your worship services. For each one you list consider:
(a) Why (historically) do we do this?
(b) What do you think they ought to 'say' to people?
(c) What do you think ordinary worshippers make of it?

So the use of signs and symbols is far from unknown in Christian tradition. Indeed back in the Middle Ages, when most people found reading a struggle, and the services as well as the Bible were all in Latin anyway, the signs and symbols were just about all that ordinary worshippers had to go on! And this has perhaps been true for most of Christian history in most places! It's a fairly late and Western innovation that worship should depend so much on written words and people being able to read and follow them.

The thing about signs and symbols is that they don't always say what you think they do! Church magazines abound with 'amusing anecdotes' about little children mistaking robed clergy for God (it's happened to me more than once), but a serious point is at stake here. Just because we think a particular picture, say of the crucifixion, is an aid to worship doesn't mean that it will be so for everyone. For one thing we have to consider that artistic taste varies widely from person to person, and for another you may read things into a picture that I don't, and perhaps that the artist never intended. So it's worth asking not just what do *we* think this symbolises, but also what will other people make of it?

The charismatic gifts

It is hardly possible to write a realistic book about worship today without giving some time to think about the influences of the charismatic movement in mainstream churches, and the use of the charismatic gifts in particular. Of course any Pentecostals reading this will rightly point out that their churches had been worshipping in this way for most of the century before the rest of us began to take any notice at all. But now that the rest of us have begun to take notice, what do we make of it all?

There is, of course, still quite a divide between those who reckon that the classical 'gifts of the Spirit' (tongues and interpretation, prophecy, gifts of healing and so on – see especially 1 Corinthians 12:8–10) are still in evident use in the church today and others who feel that such things are not to be expected as a part of modern worship. But it does appear that many churches today are open to the use of such gifts in worship, without necessarily taking on board particular ideas about what is meant by the Baptism in the Spirit or theories of inspiration.

Certainly it is true that 'charismatic worship' has given a much higher place to the expression of emotions in worship as opposed to simply the stating of facts. The far more expressive words of many modern songs and choruses, the open prayer times, the spirit of expectancy that God is not only here but is speaking to us, not just through the preacher or the hymns, but directly to our hearts; all these things involve a wider part of our being than just the mind, and surely are to be welcomed on that account.

Questions of charismatic worship

But welcoming a widening of the means of communication still needs to go alongside a serious look at what is being communicated! And there are questions to be put to churches that have welcomed charismatic expressions of worship. Some of them are listed below.

- What means is there for 'testing' the various parts of more open worship to see if they really are helpful and upbuilding – or even true?
- Are there 'unspoken rules' about what people can and can't, or do and don't say when they pray aloud or 'bring a word'? Is it always about flowing waters or burning fires? Are some areas of our Christian life not addressed? (Does God, for example, ever challenge our political choices through words of prophecy – or wouldn't he do that?)
- What images are used to speak of God, Jesus and the Spirit? Are the images in danger of becoming 'graven images', that is in limiting our vision of the greatness of God? For example, do we think nowadays more of Jesus as Lover and less as Judge? Is God totally Father but never Mother?

It is my personal belief that charismatic worship has brought a deep enrichment to modern church life,

THINK SPOT

Is charismatic worship a feature of your church's life? If not, could it have a part to play? If it is, then ask the questions above of your situation.

and one which is especially valuable in cities. It not only speaks to our emotions as well as our minds, but it is very often God who is doing the speaking. Would that this could be equally said of all the more traditional acts of worship!

Music in worship

St Augustine, the famous early Christian writer, said that he didn't know whether he valued music in worship because of the power it had to lift his soul to God or feared it because of the danger that it fixed his attention on the music and not on the God it was meant to glorify. For some people, on the other hand, music is no more than annoying twitterings, and a distraction from the serious business of worship.

The way we use music in worship, and the sorts of music we use, can exert a great influence over what we are doing. Music has the power to by-pass some of the more strictly logical parts of our minds, and touch most of us more directly at the emotional level. It's hard to describe why apparently simple, even banal, words can gain the power to inspire by virtue of the music they are set to – but for most of us it's a very real experience. Why else have the words of 'You'll never walk alone' such power to stir the heart of every Liverpool supporter? So it's worth considering what we do with music in our churches and why we do it.

THINK SPOT

Think of your favourite piece of church music. Can you put into words what it is about it that is so special to you? What does it 'say to you' about God or yourself?

Types of music

In days past there seemed to be a 'type' of music that was generally accepted as 'church music'. Whether it was Anglican chants, Wesleyan hymns or traditional choruses, it was fairly clear what was acceptable in church and what wasn't. Nowadays that has all changed. Not that the traditional types of church music have disappeared – but they have been added to by a wealth of recent song and hymn writing, in a very wide range of musical styles. Some modern hymns borrow well-known tunes from other sources, such as, for example, Richard Bewes' 'God is our strength and refuge' sung to the 'Dambusters March'. This isn't a new practice, but often seems so to those for whom secular tunes used for church music have long since acquired their own sacred 'overtones'! Other modern Christian worship songs, for example in the style associated with writers such as Graham Kendrick, are newly composed tunes which, as one musician recently remarked to me, in other times would have been used for folk ballads – and sometimes still are. Then others have been greatly helped by the music of Taize, based on making traditional plainsong chanting accessible to modern, often younger, congregations; others use the music of the Iona Community, published under the 'Wildgoose' imprint, and yet others have found spiritual encouragement in the words and music brought together in the Greenbelt Festival, which ranges from folk through traditional 'protest genre' to heavy rock, taking in much else on the way.

Personally I do not believe there is such a thing as 'sacred music', unless by that we mean music that has gained sacred associations by long familiarity of use within church contexts. But really it's all in the eye (ear?) of the beholder. The strains that to me bring back memories of Sunday afternoons at Crusader class singing, 'For God so loved the world, I find it written in verse 16, John's gospel, chapter 3...', to another call to mind happy evenings in the pub, and the more traditional words of 'Oh Danny Boy'!

All types of music used in worship have their strengths and weaknesses. Traditional hymns can be much neglected. They carry with them strong associations from people's past, they often have much stronger, and clearer, doctrinal content than modern short choruses, and many of them they can be sung with gusto by people who have real problems following the ups and downs and tempo changes of more recent worship songs, especially when played by less than experienced musicians.

On the other hand a poor pianist or organist – or congregation! – can reduce the best hymn to a dirge or a drone, and to sing nothing but hymns can be the musical equivalent of a diet composed only of suet pudding!

Modern songs and choruses come in many shapes and sizes, and it seems that they come thicker and faster each year that goes by. Certainly the songbooks come out wave upon wave, and a church that wanted to keep up with the latest music would have to spend hundreds of pounds a year buying new books and discarding their partly used old ones. Something most city churches are not in a position to do!

We have also had experience in Manchester, as have many others in the past twenty years, of using modern music forms as a means of worship. For

the sixties and seventies generation, like me, this may mean rock music and all that goes with it; for the late eighties and nineties it's as likely to be reggae and rap, or other modern styles. We started up a monthly late Sunday evening service aimed at young people with little or no church background: the content and music is largely planned by the young people under an overall 'light touch' oversight from the church leadership. Such events are mirrored elsewhere and we claimed nothing very special for ours – only that it's another answer to the ever- present need for the church to find ways of relating the gospel to a younger generation.

For some, the debate continues as to whether such music can ever be a legitimate means of Christian communication, but I am sure it can be. The harder question is whether a particular use of it actually achieves anything beyond novelty. The whole modern music ethos is so markedly different from what is traditionally expected of a church service that serious thought needs to be given to how to use the style, especially with a mixed-age congregation. It is perhaps unrealistic to expect an older generation to find it easy to worship in this way – but equally important to realise that a younger generation may find it opening the door to fresh experiences of God, in a language they can understand.

Whatever the style, as with the older hymns, some modern songs are excellent, both musically and in words; others are truly awful, and most somewhere in between. It is important that someone looks at them as they come along and asks the basic question: 'What is it that this song is inviting me to say?' It may be that you will find some that are banal in the extreme, others that are theologically unsound, and yet others that are little more than holy nonsense. But amongst the dross is much gold – and it's important to sift it out and then put it to use.

One significant trend of recent years is the number of songs inviting the singer to make statements about the way they feel about their present spiritual experience, as opposed to a former tendency to make statements about what is true about God. For all Christians, but especially those in inner-city areas, this emphasis on experience as opposed to theory can be a valuable corrective – but it does present the additional challenge of what to do if you *don't* feel what the songs says you do. It's one thing to come to church having screamed at your husband or wife or threatened to murder the kids and then be invited to affirm the truth of a Creed or statement of faith. It's quite another to come in that state of mind and immediately be invited to sing about how much you love Jesus, or to invite others to share your spiritual 'high'. What does seem to be important is the way such songs are introduced and sung through (many of them are the sort that are often repeated a number of times). Every effort needs to be made to avoid the 'coercive' approach that tries to generate the feeling by group pressure

('Now sing it one more time, as if you really mean it!'), and many people may need 'permission' from the front to 'opt out' of some songs either mentally or actually by not singing them. It's not that such songs are wrong – indeed, they can be a most valuable way of allowing people to express what they truly *do* feel. But there's a tight-rope to walk between encouraging people into truly Christian response to God, which is a proper role of worship, and bullying them into pretending to be what they aren't or feel what they don't – which is not only bad practice, but can be spiritually catastrophic.

One further thing to note is that whereas in the past the picture of our relationship with God used in songs seemed mainly to be that of 'Father/son' (as they used to put it – 'Father/child' as we ought now to learn to say), there is also a new tendancy to replace this with 'bridegroom/bride' imagery, or even 'lover/loved'. Perhaps this reflects a modern trend to recoognise the many shortcomings in our own relationships with earthly parents and a growing inability amongst some worshippers to identify with 'Father God' imagery. This is instead being replaced with 'Lover Jesus' pictures. Of course all these pictures are biblical in varying degrees, but there are questions to be asked about the suitability of songs with what can often only be described as sexual overtones. It is arguable whether a movement from 'Father' to 'Lover' imagery is always an improvement in congregations where there will be many people for whom 'love' and 'sex' have been synonymous. There is, of course, a wealth of biblical pictures to draw on if we can look a little further. For example, for many the key idea may come in John 15:15 when Jesus says: 'I do not call you servants any longer... Instead I call you friends.' Perhaps that's why Dave Cave's powerful book on his experience of church life in inner-city Liverpool is called *Jesus is my best mate*.

THINK SPOT

1 What is your impression of the types of music used in your church? Are you happy with the balance? If not, what do you feel is missing?

2 Can you think of modern songs or choruses that you would describe as 'pure gold' or else as 'holy nonsense'? Are there any you are reluctant to sing because of their content?

3 What do you think about 'feelings' songs as opposed to 'truth' songs? Can you recall good times when you have felt 'encouraged' by such songs, or bad times when you have felt 'bullied'? How can a leader of worship avoid such pitfalls?

Getting it right

Whatever the musical tradition of your church, be it a long-standing attachment to a particular hymn-book or a much more recent tradition dictated by the choruses the guitarist has learned to play – what matters is that people learn not to claim divine inspiration only for their sort of

music, whilst calling down curses on the types they happen not to like or be familiar with. Rather it is important that we ask not, 'What are we used to?' or, 'What do I like?' but instead, 'What will help this congregation worship better?'

Once this approach has been adopted there are other factors that will affect what happens musically in your church. Unlike more suburban churches, where there may be many gifted musicians to hand, inner-city congregations are often restricted as much as anything by the actual players and intruments they can call upon. It may be that an elderly organ, in dubious repair, with a willing but technically less than gifted organist, is all that is available. It may be backed up only by a guitarist who can muster not much more than half-a-dozen basic chords. In such circumstances, to try to reproduce the effect of choral evensong in King's College, or a packed meeting at Spring Harvest, would be like trying to 'do' the Last Night of the Proms as a school assembly! We must be realistic about what can be achieved! But thankfully there are a number of useful books around for reluctant organists or pianists and relatively unskilled guitarists which can help avoid such mistakes and guide us into more constructive solutions. And if it comes to it, as sometimes it will, that there's no one with any musical talent available, then some congregations find taped music good to sing along to, and others will be happy to sing simple songs unaccompanied or to say, rather than sing, some well-known hymns.

A number of churches still have church choirs whose days of former glory have long since departed, but no one has had the courage to retire the faithful remnant with appropriate thanks. Such groups, often seated well apart from the rest of the congregation, sometimes robed, can have the opposite effect of what is intended. They remove the few strong singers from the body of the congregation and in doing so discourage them from any attempt at making even a joyful, let alone a tuneful, noise to the Lord. Choirs can be valuable, but only if they are in sufficient numbers, well led and rehearsed, and see themselves as serving the congregation, not giving a performance. Many churches also have some form of 'music group'. These are usually distinguished from choirs by the type of music they sing, where they sit, what they wear and the instruments that accompany them. But that being said, just about all the questions that apply to choirs apply equally to such groups.

And in a number of churches there are both choirs and music groups. This can work well, especially if there is good communication between the two, but more often than not it is a recipe for rivalry and confusion. The net result is that the worship is what suffers. Better by far to have one integrated group combining the best of both approaches. If that isn't possible, then at least to have one accepted and acknowledged leadership structure under which both groups sit equally and fairly.

Indeed, what is crucial whatever your set-up is that there is someone who is responsible for the music of the church. In smaller churches it may be the minister who takes on this overall responsibility; in more traditional churches it is a choirmaster, in others a music group leader. Ideally a system of co-leadership can provide the mutual support and breadth of vision that this ministry needs. But whoever it is, it is also very important that they are clearly identified, their job is well defined, and that their relationship with the other leadership structures of the church is clear and known. Music in worship is too important to be left to the whims of an independent dictatorship, whatever name it goes under!

THINK SPOT

1 Who decides about the music that is used in your worship? Who do they discuss it with? Who are they answerable to in the church leadership? If there aren't clear answers to these questions, would you benefit from raising them with your church's governing body or council?

2 Try and write down (if it hasn't already been done) a 'Job Description' for your choir or music group. Then test it against what actually happens. If there's significant differences, what can/should be done about that?

Summing it up

Jesus said the 'greatest and most important commandment' is to, 'Love the Lord you God with all your heart, with all your soul, and with all your mind' (Matthew 22:37). Worship that is not from the heart and soul as well as the mind is worship that falls short of this ideal. By keeping God at arms length, it fails to seek 'God in my world' – and so, unsurprisingly, will have difficulty in finding him there!

City Christians, who for better or worse have learned more than most about living on their emotions, can therefore be closer to the spirit of true worship than those elsewhere in the Western world. The challenge to worship leaders is to enable true worship from the heart, rather than stifle it or replace it with some manufactured synthetic.

Chapter 7

WORSHIP IN MY LANGUAGE

It is a thing plainly repugnant to the Word of God and to the custom of the Primitive Church, to have publick Prayer in the Church, or to minister the Sacraments in a tongue not understanded of the people.

(Article 24 of the 39 Articles of Religion)

The Reformers had it right. They were sure that what went on in church should be understandable to the ordinary person. That's why number 24 of the 39 Articles of the Anglican church reads as it does. Of course, the irony is that the sixteenth century language of the Articles, Prayer Book and Authorised Version has itself become 'a tongue not understanded of the people'. Take Fred and Sue, for example…

To many of our neighbours what goes on in church is a closed book. And since they may not even be sold on books in the first place, that's the way they intend to keep it. Closed. But now and then, for all sorts of reasons, Fred and Sue, or Christine will find themselves coming along to a service. What do they find when they get there?

This great debate about modern language in church is something of a modern one! For a long time it was just assumed that when you spoke to God you had a special way of speaking – just as you'd put on your best clothes when the vicar came and show him into the front room.

Fred and Sue were a young couple with a marriage problem. They'd tried all sorts of ways to sort it out, and as a last resort Sue suggested they call in the local vicar. Fred rang him, in fear and trembling. When Mike, the vicar, called round, he found them only too ready to talk about their problem – and interested in coming to church as well. But neither had ever been to church since their own baptisms in infancy. Sue had liked hymns at school assembly – Fred hadn't. Apart from that, they hadn't the foggiest what to expect… But they didn't expect to understand it. 'It'll probably do us some good though, won't it, Mike?'.

Christine was a single mum. Young Kirsty was getting on a bit and both Chris and her Mum felt that it was high time the baby was 'done'. Trouble was, they'd heard that the local minister was keen on people actually turning up to church first before fixing the date – and she knew what church was like. You sat there bored out of your skull whilst some chap woffled on in olde Englishe for over an hour. Could she cope with it? she asked herself.

That special way of speaking might be written down in a book – like the Book of Common Prayer, mainstay of Anglican worship from the 1660s to the 1960s. For Roman Catholics it was a real foreign language, Latin – and no one except the really educated had a hope of understanding it, even if the priest did speak up enough for you to hear. And for some others it was just the long words, the 'thees' and 'thous', the 'we wouldest that thou mightest' and all that – as if talking to God was like writing a letter to a foreign embassy or being summoned to an audience with the Queen.

In recent years most churches have been changing, and 'modern language services' are all the thing. Catholics use English not Latin; Anglicans have their Alternative Service Book; and others with written books have also updated them. Even those whose worship is more unwritten have adjusted their speech – a bit less of the 'waiting on the ineffable throne of grace', a bit more of the 'Thanks very much, God'.

Opinions vary about how far we should go in this line. Some find it difficult to worship in what they call 'the language of the supermarket'. Personally I've had some pretty good conversations with God in the supermarket, but I can see that what's OK for me might not be right for the full congregation assembled in all its glory on a Sunday.

Others say that it matters very much that when we come to worship we aren't tempted to put on a 'Sunday-best face', including a 'Sunday-best language', and that God will understand

THINK SPOT

Should the language we use in worship be a bit different from 'everyday' talk, because the God we worship is far greater than the merely everyday, or should it be as ordinary as possible, because it's in the ordinariness of life that he wants us to come to him?

Go through the written and spoken parts of a recent Sunday morning service and ask yourself where the language used helped you and where it didn't – and why.

us best if we talk in whatever way comes naturally to us. But I have occasionally cringed at the way some people address the Lord of all creation as if they're having a quiet giggle with a pal. And clearly you can go too far: I don't think the richly expletive laden language of the average workplace would exactly go down a treat in church.

THINK SPOT

How do those who usually lead worship in your church speak? Do they have a noticeable accent to you? And if they do, does it help you or annoy you? And would you expect someone, say reading a lesson, to have special training to get over any problems in this line? What sort of training? Who should do it?

East Enders at the East End?

There's another question beyond that of modern language. Most inner-city areas have their own variety of local speech, accent or dialogue that isn't quite the Queen's English. As the Manchester survey quoted in chapter three suggests, some people think it's good that those leading or taking part in worship speak as slowly and clearly and with as neutral an accent as possible – so everyone has a good chance of understanding. On the other hand others value their local way of speaking, and don't see why they should put on some other way of speaking just because not all present can make them out as well as others.

Perhaps that's a fair price to pay for more local people having a chance to join in leading. Either way, if local people *are* to join in leading worship, how far can we expect them to attend elocution classes before they begin? Or is accent a totally different matter from clarity?

Books

How many books and bits of paper does your church hand out when people come in? Or how many are waiting there on the pew or chair for them? Many people in inner-cities are non-readers – that's not to say they are illiterate, or can't read, but that by and large they don't read. A tabloid newspaper maybe. Perhaps the odd paperback Western or Romance. And that's it. Of course you're different. You must be to be reading this book now. But take a look at how print-heavy our worship often is. A hymn-book. A chorus book. A Bible. A notice sheet. A special announcement slip. A 'visitor slip' to fill in. Is there any way round it?

There are some ways of cutting down on paper. Maybe you should agree to stick to one song book, even though that means limiting yourselves a bit in what you sing. There's always the overhead projector of course – but don't forget to obtain copyright permission for all those songs you write out for it! And badly written words on a distant screen can be even worse than a large book in your hand. Does the service book need to be so large or wordy? The Anglican ASB is little better than the old Prayer Book for number of words and pages – although at least the print is a little larger! Home-made service books can be good – or they can be very awful! At the least they should have pictures in, should have a bright attractive cover, and shouldn't crowd too many words onto the pages. Maybe we should go all the way and abandon books altogether and just 'let the Spirit lead' the worship? On the other hand, without printed words, how can people join in together in anything? But if the words are always the same, isn't there a danger of dulling by repetition?

Here we get into the wider question of what sort of liturgical pattern of worship you favour, also discussed in chapter five. It's worth repeating that there's something to be said for many approaches – including those that aren't your own! Those who favour a freer approach might remember that freedom can often lead to monotonous 'unwritten liturgies', either of the 'leader of the day' or the supposedly free congregation where actually a certain few regularly contribute along broadly predictable lines whilst the rest keep quiet and lay odds on who's going to pray up next. Those who favour a

THINK SPOT
Are all the books and bits of paper you give people necessary? How can you cut down without losing out on the variety of provision available?

more structured approach might care to reflect on the fact that the utter predictability of a written liturgy can be no less tedious for it's being very old or produced by a very important body! And both approaches must be judged against our definition of worship: does it help me bring my world to God, and find God in my world?

Finally, think of Bibles for a moment. It used to be a test of a good evangelical church either that the worshippers all arrived clutching their leather-bound Bibles under their arms, or else that pew Bibles were provided for all. But the sight of all those word-filled Bibles can be a bit intimidating for some. At least let's not give them out at the door. And if we encourage the use of one standard version it does have the advantage that you can announce page numbers, not books and chapters – not a lot of people know where Habbakuk comes! And remember to give time for people to find the place!

The place of the clergy

'He takes a lovely service' used to be the sort of accolade the ordinary faithful gave to their favoured clergy. After all, isn't that what they're there for? Why else do we pay them all that money and give them that house to live in? ('Pity about the size and draughts, but it's a calling isn't it?')

But is it the minister's job to 'take the service'? What about everyone else? Have they a part to play beyond sitting there taking it all in – or not as the case may be? There's a great danger we reduce an 'act of worship' to just that – a 'performance' by just one actor, applauded (or not) by the audience in their seats.

The truth is that true worship is far

from just a 'performance'; but granted that there's some truth in this way of looking at it, there are in fact several ways 'ordinary members' of the congregation can join in worship:

- they can be offered a 'bit part' up front (eg read a lesson, help with communion, lead some prayers).
- they can be given a 'starring role' (eg preach the sermon, or lead the whole service).
- they can help write the script – churches with active worship committees (by any name) are usually at least part-way into this sort of involvement.
- they can improvise a part – as in churches where freedom is given for open congregational participation such as 'open prayer'.

In truth we are all 'actors' in the worship – that is we are all supposed to be active, taking part in whatever is going on, be it prayer, singing, listening or whatever. And so ideally we are all joining in, giving ourselves 100% to all that is going on about us, without ever needing to leave our seat!

But for lay involvement of the sort just listed to happen as well demands a minister and a congregation who recognise that ministry is not about 'doing it all yourself'.

So does the minister have any special role in leading worship? Of course – but it's no longer to do it all himself, as in the days when the parish priest was the only even half-educated man in the village. Rather he or she should be a trained and experienced person who enables the rest of the congregation to worship better.

This can be done in a number of ways, eg:

- helping people understand better what it is they're doing when they come to worship.
- inviting people to take on specific tasks in worship – like reading or praying.
- encouraging people when they do participate and, if necessary, seeing they get a bit of help.
- keeping the whole thing 'on the rails', doctrinally speaking.

Pete was a young trainee minister, invited to take a service in a local church while John, the regular minister, was away. 'Don't worry about the prayers', John had said. 'They'll join in if you invite them to.' So when Pete got to that point in the service he invited the congregation to suggest items for prayer. There was a pause. Then an elderly lady arose from the choir stalls. 'Young man,' she intoned, 'I thought that was what you are here for.'

THINK SPOT

Is there a group of people in your church responsible for planning or leading worship? If not – should there be? If there is – who decides what they can and can't do? How representative are they of the ordinary congregation? How representative of the local community?

- the minister may well 'preside' at most services – but certainly needn't do so on every occasion.

Readings and prayers

There's a lovely passage about the reading of the scriptures in Nehemiah chapter 8. The people of Israel have rebuilt the walls of Jerusalem, under the leadership of Nehemiah, and are resettling the city and surrounding areas as God's people once more. So they want to seal the covenant by a reading of the Law of Moses, which they do. Ezra the scribe oversees it, and when the Law is explained to the people they rejoice in it, being told in a well known verse: 'the joy of the Lord is your strength' (Nehemiah 8:10 NIV).

But have you ever tried using it as a reading in church? It's fine up to verse 4 – then comes the trouble. A whole list of unpronounceable Hebrew names of Ezra's assistants, both there and in verse 7. A member of our church called to read the passage just gave up on it and read them out as 'and all that lot too'!

Reading the Scriptures is a vital part of our worship. Whatever else goes on in the service, it anchors us firmly back into God's revelation to us. But as we've seen above, it may not all be plain sailing. Many people are shy of helping worship in this way because they think they'd 'get it wrong'.

Of course not everyone has the gift of being able to read aloud– but many more could have than think they do! Here's a few simple rules that will help almost anyone get it right enough.

THINK SPOT

Which people read from the Bible in services in your church? Should others be asked? If so – who by? Do they need a bit of help in it? Who is best to give it? Can you add any more DOs and DON'Ts to the list above?

- DON'T think that the Bible has to be read in a special 'holy' voice.
- DO think about what you're reading and try to put natural meaning into it.
- DON'T panic and trip over your tongue.
- DO speak up, speak slowly, and stop for a breather if you get stuck.
- DON'T be frightened of any microphones your church uses.
- DO speak up anyway. They can always turn you down – but it may be harder to turn you up.

Keeping quiet!

We're funny about silence in church, aren't we? On the one hand some people seem to think the place is so sacred that anything above a whisper is sacrilege. That's certainly what lay behind the attitude Yvonne and Paul met with. On the other hand we can talk, sing, pray or otherwise gabble our way through the service so loudly that you never get a chance to stop and think at all.

In a lot of inner-city areas silence is pretty hard to come by. City life can be

Yvonne and Paul had come along to church for the baptism of their new niece, Colette. They'd brought Marcus and Gloria with them – well you could hardly leave two pre-schoolers at home alone could you? During the service the kids got a bit restless and at last the minister stopped the service and suggested that 'If you can't keep the children quiet you'd better leave the building so as not spoil it for everyone else'. That was the last time Yvonne and Paul went to church.

one long noise – from the non-stop free pop concert from your neighbours' ghetto blaster through those too-thin walls, to the midnight screams of the latest drunken fights on the way home from the pub. From the shouts of the kids playing out on the streets till late, to the ever-present background roar of traffic on the main roads, or far from background for those unlucky enough to live next to the inner ring-road! Noise pollution invades our heads, scrambles our thoughts and distracts our prayers. So it seems a pity we waste the opportunities for silence that church gives on 'holy hushes', but don't use it to create space for God to speak in that 'still, small voice'.

There are plenty of chances to use silences well in church services. At the beginning, before launching into that first rousing hymn. As a prelude to confession, to give opportunity to recollect just what it is you're supposed to be saying Sorry for today. During prayers, to give a chance to listen as well as speak to God. After a reading, to let it sink in rather than be instantly forgotten. After a sermon, to ask God to underline in your mind that one thing he's got to say to you from it. And many others besides.

THINK SPOT

How much silence do you use in your worship? Is it introduced or does it just happen?

How do you feel about outside noises creeping in – people's small children, or those loud motorbikes on the street outside?

And silences needn't be mingy little fifteen seconders. A whole minute is surprisingly valuable. Several minutes can work wonders as you get used to it. As long as the person leading warns you in advance of course – so you don't just think they've lost their place, or forgotten to look at their watch, or gone to sleep.

Silences are the same in anybody's language. Maybe the language of heaven will be less eternal songs and hymns of fellowship, more extended quiet!

When the Lamb broke open the seventh seal, there was silence in heaven for about half an hour.

(Revelation 8:1)

Summing it up

The way we talk to God tells us something about how we think of him. Serious, solemn language and silence can remind us that he's great, exalted and not just 'one of us'. Ordinary, chatty language and enthusiastic loud songs or shouts can remind us that he loves us, is interested in us and wants us to come naturally to him with our concerns.

In the city the second way of speaking probably comes more easily to us. As we 'bring our world to God' we will want to talk about it in the sort of language we use in our world. We should not be ashamed to use such language in worship – indeed we should actually revel in the fact that it's helping us closer to understanding part of the nature of the God we serve. But maybe as we look to 'find God in our world', we sometimes also need to work a bit harder at remembering the sort of things about God that the first way of speaking would remind us of. At the end of the day, what matters most is not so much how we talk to God as what we're actually saying!

Chapter 8

KALEIDOSCOPIC WORSHIP

Who is in the kaleidoscope?

City areas vary widely between one another, and a lot of what this chapter has to say may not be relevant to someone whose area or congregation is monochrome in nature – for example a large overspill estate or some inner-area redevelopments. If that describes you then you may find it less frustrating to skip most of this chapter and return to it later. Although if you do, you may miss out on some interesting insights by the way!

In many city areas an exciting factor of daily life is the variety of people all about you. Certainly it's been true of my own experience of life in inner Manchester that the breadth of cultures, backgrounds and lifestyles present is far greater than anything I'd known previously, growing up in more 'comfortable Britain'.

In the part of Manchester I lived in, for example, are local Mancunians born and bred, as well as people who have moved into the city from elsewhere in Britain, either fellow Northerners or those from the distant South, beyond Watford. Then there is a strong Irish community, and a significant minority of Polish background.

A significant group is of West Indian origin, mainly from Jamaica, but also from other Caribbean islands. The generation who came to this country as welcome guests in the fifties and early sixties are now increasingly ageing and a number have returned home to live out their final days in retirement there. They are the ones who faced the immediate racial prejudice and hostility, later turning to more institutional racism once the economic conditions made them no longer so welcome; government controls on immigration both echoed and fuelled the popular racism evidenced in calls from some to 'send them all back where they came from'. But of course the more significant group for the future are their children and grandchildren, who are for the most part British-born black people for whom this country is the only home they have known – and yet where they often face as much prejudice as their parents ever did.

The West Indian community shared a Christian tradition with the country they came to – indeed they soon discovered that their allegiance to the church was far greater than that of many citizens of the so-called 'Christian motherland' – but a later group of arrivals did not share this common religious heritage. For there's also a large Asian population, mainly Muslims from northern India and Pakistan, but with a significant number of Sikhs also. Such people have found and still find it harder to cross the additional barriers of language and religion as well as culture and custom, and so have tended to group more together in self-contained, closed communities, centred around one of the two mosques or the one gurdwara.

In recent years Asian people also have been gaining in self-confidence and joining more in community life, presenting new questions to white 'Christian' Britain as we take on board the fact that in the innner-city at least – and indeed throughout the country if we would but see it – we are now a multi-racial, multi-cultural and multi-faith Britain.

All this is reasonably 'typical' of many city, especially inner-city, areas. It all adds to the rich diversity of cultural and religious expression to be found. And that then begins to raise questions about worship and witness for the church which this chapter will try to address.

THINK SPOT

How much do you know about the different ethnic groups that make up your church's neighbourhood? How well does your congregation reflect them?

'If you're black or if you're white...'

'...if you're fat or lean: God loves you.' So begins a chorus sung by many who have encountered the Manchester–based but nationally travelling Children's Christian Crusade. True as the words are, taken at face value, they could also be said to sum up an attitude common among many Christian people today, that issues of race are irrelevant to the true message of the gospel. 'We're all the same under the skin,' we're told. God isn't colour-prejudiced and therefore as his children neither are we. The best thing we can do about colour is put it out of our minds. We are to be 'colour-blind' in our approach. Surely this is the most Christian thing to do?

The trouble with this approach is that it fails to reckon with the fact that although God may not be influenced by the colour of a person's skin, most people are! In actual fact to be 'colour-blind', however well-meaning the phrase, is half-way to being totally blind – blind to all the differences of culture and background that colour usually signifies, and the attitudes of prejudice and discrimination that it usually brings on. There is a vital distinction here which it is important to get hold of. In themselves racial and colour differences have absolutely no significance before God; we are created equal; equally sinners; equally redeemable. Those who suggest or believe that distinctive racial and national characteristics have anything other than temporary and human significance, let alone that they indicate any 'natural' superiority or inferiority, are defying basic truth about humankind that the Bible teaches us. In *that* sense, and in that sense alone, we not only can but must be 'colour-blind' in our attitudes to one another.

However, in the context of past history and of present prejudice, racial and national differences mean a whole lot of things. There is the whole shameful history of the oppression and exploitation of black people by white to take into account – and the way our present attitudes are still shaped by it. We proudly state that the slave trade was abolished after pressure from Wilberforce and other prominent Christians, but conveniently ignore the fact that for many years it was as spiritedly defenced by many *on Christian grounds.* Many still prefer to close their eyes and ears to the solid evidence of the reality of racial disadvantage in Britain, when study after study shows that to be black in Britain today means to be discriminated against in housing, employment, education, before the law and so on. Then there are the unguarded comments that otherwise apparently educated and liberal-minded people come out with in what they apparently consider to be 'safe' company. I well recall the shock I felt as I sat in the General Synod cafeteria and heard another member comment, in passing, that we were 'about to debate the "nig-nogs" again'!

THINK SPOT

'A proper Christian response to questions of racial difference is...to challenge each and every attitude of prejudice and seek to alter each and every instance of injustice arising out of people's perceptions of colour.'

How would you compare your church's approach to racial matters with that view? Is there anything you would like to see changing?

All these things are evident reminders to those with eyes and ears to see and hear that racial prejudice and racism (which can be defined as prejudice in action) are as real a factor in modern British society as respect for the monarchy or the love of football. But a good deal more destructive than either! It is therefore naive in the extreme to pretend that we can invite black people to function in society as if none of these things were true. In *that* sense, a pretended 'colour-blindness' may simply mean an unwillingness to open our eyes to the reality of others', and our own, prejudices!

Rather, a proper Christian response to questions of racial difference is not to pretend that they don't exist, but to challenge each and every attitude of prejudice and seek to alter each and every instance of injustice arising out of people's perceptions of colour.

So in what ways can churches make that challenge, in particular viewing the matter, as we are doing, in the context of worship? We shall begin by looking at some recent history.

Black-led churches

The first factor to confront us is the existence in many cities of what tend to be known as black or black-led churches, with their own distinctive styles of worship and patterns of church life. We looked briefly at a 'typical' one of these in the early parts of chapter three.

The history of black-led churches in this country is short but relatively little-known amongst white Christians. Many of those coming into this country from the Carribbean after the war were already practising Christians and they came from countries where religion still had a much more integral part in the social fabric of life than it did in disillusioned post-war Britain. The first thing to strike such Christians, as personal story after personal story bears witness, was the religious indifference of the majority of British people and the personal coldness of the minority who did attend church. A common experience was to seek out the nearest church of one's own denomination – Anglican, Methodist, Roman Catholic or whatever – only to be ostracised by the other (white) worshippers. Indeed often people were asked not to return, or told that 'your church is down the road'. For indeed, in the light of this reaction, many black Christians had taken instead to reproducing the 'house meeting' approach to fellowship familiar from back home. Such house meetings began to increase in number, to outgrow their homes and to seek premises in rented halls, and eventually to buy up old church buildings no longer needed by their white counterparts. And although many Caribbean Christians came to this country as members of existing 'mainstream' churches, others came as members of American-based Pentecostal or Holiness churches, such as the Church of God. These were the churches that grew fast, as house churches affiliated to them, and although they grew also by division and splinter-groups, throughout the sixties and seventies and into the eighties their spectacular growth became remarked upon as the one encouraging sign in inner-city Christianity, which otherwise seemed generally in retreat. Alongside them, especially latterly, has come the growth of churches drawn more from an African tradition, formed by similar processes but amongst those coming to this country from Africa rather than the Caribbean. They became collectively known as the 'black-led churches', although often the parent bodies back in the States were and are primarily white.

Alongside this sorry tale of rejection, it is true that there were also welcome exceptions; that some black Christians were not so easily daunted and opted to stick with their original churches come what may, and in due course some others were won for Christ and joined mainstream churches in the 'ordinary' way. So today in inner-cities it is not uncommon to find churches of various sorts alongside one another: there are the all-white churches; there are 'mainstream' churches with a number of black worshippers, either smaller or larger, although usually not correspondingly reflected in the leadership structures; and there are the black-led churches, normally with a very high proportion of black members. What there often is not is real communication between these churches, even when they are close neighbours. So myths and stereotypes abound about 'white' and 'black' worship – not necessarily helped by the limited exposure to set-piece worship given by 'Songs of Praise'-type programmes from the 'other' tradition.

A challenge

All this presents very real challenges to churches that are majority white or majority black in areas where the actual racial mix is more cosmopolitan. Put simply it is: Are we content for our churches to mirror the divisions of society, or is there a vision of the church which calls us beyond this to challenge these divisions, and to seek to build churches which are truly multi-racial in composition? For there is a school of thought that would seek to encourage this development of churches divided on racial grounds in a form of ecclesiastical apartheid, arguing that people most like to come to faith in an environment similar to their own. This line of thought, tempting as it seems in terms of 'results', is one I would challenge as being essentially limited in outlook and being expressly challenged by the gospel. The New Testament makes it clear that the church created by response to the liberating gospel is intended to model a new society – indeed a new humanity – in which such divisions of class, race and culture are neither ignored nor pandered to, but overcome. This is a much harder course of action than the alternatives. But in the end I am sure it is the only one which is true to the nature of the gospel itself.

Worshipping together

It is against this backdrop that we are to look at how our worship can contribute to and be enriched by the multi-racial composition of many inner-city areas. I have four suggestions, born out of practical experience.

1 'Black-led' and 'mainstream' churches must begin to worship together wherever possible. This needs to be far more than the occasional joint jamboree, although that has its place as a starting point. But to really worship together we need to learn to know one another as individuals, and that comes from longer-term and deeper exposure to one another. Only then can we begin to be freed from racial stereotypes in worship as in any other sphere of life. In our area what began as occasional shared prayer-meetings has led to a fruitful partnership whereby the leadership groups of three churches meet on a regular quarterly basis to share experiences and plan common mission strategies to our neighbourhood. It has taken a number of years to reach this point, however, and even now many of our church members are only marginally involved.

2 Black members of white-led churches must be affirmed in their place in the congregation. Too often it is the whites who 'run' the church, the blacks who have things 'done to' them. Because they may be polite and have learned patience the hard way, black Christians will often take a lot of messing around from their white fellow believers, but once a minister or other church leader begins to seriously listen to what such members really feel and think, they should be prepared for some surprises. There is often a wealth of spirituality and talent buried beneath an apparently quiet exterior. But also, often, a wealth of hurts! I am aware of one black church member who had such hurtful things said when he had been persuaded to be an office-holder that he had vowed never again to expose himself to such treatment from his fellow-Christians!

In our own congregation, we first addressed this when our three black church council members called a meeting simply for the black church members, the only white person present being myself as minister. Arising from this were several recommendations which the church council then agreed – though not without some dissent! But at least white Christians were trying to listen to what black Christians had to say, and not deciding for them what is best for them.

3 Black Christians should be listened to, not just talked about. A besetting sin of those who begin to realise there is a issue here, and one which I am obviously in danger of myself at this point, is for white Christians to become 'experts' on what black Christians really want. There is no substitute for learning to listen before you speak. And in doing so you will discover, of course, that there is no such thing as 'the black view', any more than there is 'the white view'. Individuals differ and their opinions differ, and so do their depths of spirituality. Colour need not be relevant to that.

4 Worship that takes race seriously will also take racial justice seriously. Our God is a God of justice and many injustices have been heaped upon black people, in both ancient and recent history. Challenging injustice is part of the worship of our lives – and as such should also form part of the worship of our Sunday services! Our prayers, our words, our concerns as reflected in the preaching and songs, should be able to be measured against what they say about our commitment to racial justice – and indeed justice of all sorts – and if found wanting should be changed. For example, the present state and operation of immigration and nationality law provides many situations where Christians have felt obliged to challenge the state on behalf of their brothers and sisters.

An example of this came when a Ghanaian member of another local church was threatened with deportation, together with her infant son, born in this country. A number of us became convinced that the right course was to support this mother and child in their appeal for the exercise of compassionate discretion to stay, but it was significant how many other Christians felt uneasy at allying themselves with people of other faiths or none in an apparently anti-establishment protest. Following Jesus will sometimes mean coming down off the fence, and in strange company – but some of the most powerful worship I have experienced came as we sang songs around a brazier outside the Community Sanctuary at Victoria's house at the daily prayer meetings. Ultimately the Home Office conceded and allowed her to stay: a notable victory had been won by Christians standing together with others on the side of the oppressed and against injustice.

I've written more about the story of this campaign in an issue of *Racial Justice*, the magazine of Evangelical Christians for Racial Justice. This organisation can provide resources, both written and people, to help Christians look more seriously at their own approach to issues of race and justice from a biblical perspective. ECRJ can be contacted at their Birmingham office at 12 Bell Barn Shopping Centre, Cregoe Street, Birmingham B15 2DZ.

THINK SPOT

1 How divided along racial grounds are the churches in your community? What opportunities are there for black and white Christians to worship together?
2 If your church is to any degree multi-racial, how far do the people visibly leading worship on Sundays reflect that diversity?
3 Are your prayers marked by a commitment to racial justice? Do you think they should be?
4 What would be/is the reaction in your congregation about supporting involvement in issues of racial justice?

People of other faiths

People of other faiths present rather different challenges to us. It may seem that a book mainly about worship can have little to say about this, but there are some important areas to consider. A basic question that faces Christians when confronted by other faiths in Britain today is: 'What should be our attitude to these people?' Broadly speaking there are three types of approach on offer:

- to see their faith as totally wrong and even evil and to seek, in theory and perhaps also in practice, to convert them to Christianity as we understand it.

This might be called the 'traditional' view, although there is plenty in Christian tradition that takes a different approach. Although it preserves a clear understanding of the uniqueness of the Christian faith, it is open to all sorts of charges of narrow-mindedness, failure to appreciate the good in others, and a limited appreciation of the way God is at work within his whole creation.

- to see their faith, in its purest and best form, as a way of life and of salvation quite on a level with our own and, in some ways, even superior to it. We can, perhaps, learn from one another, but there should be no question of conversion.

This can be called the 'modern' view and in seeking to be open to what God is doing in other faiths it would seem to abandon any distinctive Christian claims, and in doing so to sit very lightly to the New Testament witness to the faith.

- to see their faith as a means by which God has revealed truth to them, doubtless, as is our own, mixed with other things less good, but to hold fast to the belief that Jesus Christ is God's only way of salvation so that although people may perhaps be saved without knowledge of Christ they cannot be saved without the work of Christ.

This 'in–between' view is closest to what I myself think to be true, and allows us both to look for truth in another faith whilst reserving the belief that God's saving truth is found in Christianity alone.

Whichever of these views we adopt is bound to influence not only our attitude to other faiths in principle but how we treat them in practice, including in our worship. Areas where this is likely to arise include the following:

Prayers for the local community

Here we will need to consider whether we regard people of other faiths as proper subjects for our prayer, apart from prayers for their conversion. For example, suppose local Asian families have recently been the subject of racially-motivated attacks – how likely are we to give space for that in our prayers (and for those who carry out the attacks of course)?

Prayers about evangelism, locally and overseas

Many Christians will still feel that it is a natural thing to pray for the conversion of their neighbours of other faiths. If this is so we need to ask ourselves how open we can be about the possibility that they have things to teach us as well as us having a gospel to share with them. When the other-faith community is also a minority group in the overall national context, perhaps feeling its very identity is under threat, it can be very easy for our genuine concern and prayer for conversion to slide into cultural imperialism, or for the language we use to imply things we may not mean.

Prayer for 'the nation'

There is a particular danger here that when Christians pray for 'our nation' we have in mind a white, Anglo-Saxon and Protestant nation. The undoubted fact that we have such a recent past ought not to blind us to the fact that the present reality is rather different. 'Our nation' is now made up of people of varying religions, and mostly of none. It is not good enough to echo prayers that 'call the nation back to God' when for many people they have either never been with God or their understanding of God is vastly different from our own. In particular it will not do to borrow phrases and verses from the history of Israel in the Old Testament, a state where church and nation *were* one and the same, and apply them to Britain today – as some are apt to do. Since the New Testament, there never has been a time when a nation and its church have been one and the same, even if sometimes it was more possible to pretend it than others.

School worship

Although strictly beyond our immediate brief, this is nonetheless an area many Christians will find themselves involved in, whether as parents, teachers or via governing bodies. What has always been a problematical area is made much more so since the advent of the 1988 Education Reform Act, which not only put a renewed emphasis on the daily collective worship that has always been required in schools, but also ruled that such worship shall be 'wholly or mainly of a broadly Christian character' – unless a school and its Local Authority agree to make a specific exception in their case. This raises a number of important issues, such as:

- is compulsory collective worship a contradiction in terms?
- how can someone be asked to lead worship if they have no clearly worked-out faith of their own?
- how does a strengthened emphasis on Christianity work in multi-faith areas, particularly when significant numbers of Muslim children are present?

Christians involved in leading such 'acts of worship' need to think long and hard about what they want to do, and also about what is fair to impose on a captive audience. It is worth asking ourselves how we would feel if the tables were turned and children from Christian homes were being subjected to compulsory worship of a 'broadly Muslim character'.

Inter-faith worship

This is a growing possibility in some areas and offers us a whole new set of questions. When the Pope invited leaders of many world religions to Assisi to pray with him for world peace, was he offering a dramatic and bold lead, or falling into a subtle but fatal trap? When invited to attend worship at the Sikh gurdwara do you stay away, attend but spiritually cross your fingers, or try to say your prayers to the accompaniment of their singing? If you are asked, as I have been, into a Muslim home to pray against the evil spirit that is said to have caused a 'cot death', do you pray in Jesus' name and, if so, do you invite them to join with you? All these are real questions to which there are not easy answers. Or rather, one person's easy answer is another's hard-hearted attitude or else soft-headed compromise!

I feel that to worship *alongside* a person of another faith need not be a problem, but to seek shared worship *with* them may well be. But it would depend on what was in that act of worship. Prayers of thanks for the birth of a child may readily be offered despite differing understandings of the

THINK SPOT

1 Are there people of other faiths in your local community in any number? If not, what do you feel the above section has to teach you?

2 Which of the five 'difficult areas' above is the most problematical for you personally? What do you agree with in what has been said about it? What do you disagree with? Why?

God who is receiving them; any prayer that tended to diminish the unique significance of Christ in God's plan of salvation will present difficulties for most Christians.

Upstairs/Downstairs?

The final cultural difference I want to look at under this heading is one that is often closely related to race, but is also significantly different and of wider application – the question of class. Some people suggest that Britain today is moving towards being a classless society. There may be some truth in this in terms of a direction, but it is still more true that most people can instinctively define themselves as either 'middle-class' or 'working-class' (or perhaps more commonly, 'ordinary people').

So far this book has been written on the assumption that certain things are broadly true of city congregations which are not true, or less so, of people elsewhere. And if we replaced 'city' by 'working-class' not a lot would probably need to be changed. But the fact is that many, perhaps most, city congregations are not solidly working-class, and indeed some are solidly very far from that! So what we are actually aiming to do in worship is to meet the needs of people who are often very different from one another, but who sit there side by side and look to worship leaders to offer something all can equally benefit from. It can be a dauntingly tall order.

If this is your situation, then it will probably affect everything you do in worship, but there is a key area where it becomes especially acute, and so it's preaching that we'll look at now.

Middle-class, perhaps university-educated, people will probably be happy with longer more 'organised' sermons. They will tend to expect them to follow closely through a biblical text, verse by verse, or perhaps to explore all aspects of a topic. Working-class people will tend to be more concerned that the sermon hits them between the eyes, that it is well illustrated, with examples appropriate to their lives, and above all, as an inner-city minister friend of mine says, that the preacher learns how to THINK VISUAL!

Meeting these differing expectations means hard work and creative thinking. Most ministers or preachers, whatever their original backgrounds, have been well schooled in middle-class ways and need a leap of imagination to understand what all groups in the congregation are looking for, and the ability to deliver it.

Useful ideas I have seen or put into practice include:

- acting out a Bible passage rather than reading it – this obviously demands a degree of preparation but often less than might be imagined, as a 'polished performance' is less important than enthusiasm and commitment. I have found you can often 'coach as you go along', especially (but not only) with children!
- telling a story as one of the characters in it, rather than as a dispassionate 'third party'. This might be called the 'David Kossoff' approach, and with a little boldness and imagination can be very effective.
- encouraging feedback from the congregation during a sermon (This can back-fire if you find you can't *stop* the feedback!)
- breaking up into smaller groups to discuss particular questions arising out of what's been said. The thing to look for here is the sort of questions that will enable anyone who wants to have a say to do so; the thing to avoid here is any tedious 'reporting back' at length!

Whilst considering preaching we ought to stop and ask who does it. Traditionally some churches have limited this to those who have won their way through a long apprenticeship and a course involving much academic study. Others have been willing to 'open the pulpit' to anyone who might have a 'message to bring'. Each approach has its dangers! But it seems important that city churches go to lengths to discover and encourage potential preachers from within the ranks of their ordinary members, and give them opportunities to 'try out' their skills in less threatening situations before being thrown in the deep end of, say, a Sunday morning family service!

What does matter is that preachers have some way of knowing how their sermons are being received by the congregation. One way of doing this, if there are several people in a church who preach, is for them to meet on a regular basis for mutual encouragement and criticism (in that order!). It also helps if it is said from time to time that comments beyond the 'lovely sermon vicar' variety are appreciated – both positive and less so.

THINK SPOT

1 Who decides who preaches in your church? Who 'encourages and criticises' the preachers? Do you think it works well?

2 Can you encourage your preachers (perhaps you are one!) to explore more of the sorts of 'non–middle–class' ways of preaching mentioned above?

3 What are the views in your church over the matters listed under 'Other Differences' above?

Other differences

Of course differences of outlook and approach based on class will show themselves in many other ways in city churches, but for the most part these will not so readily be classified under the heading of worship. But it may be worth considering how your church is affected by differing views on such matters as:

- the clothes you wear to worship in.
- the time you arrive for church, and how acceptable it is to wander in and out during a service.
- noise levels during services.
- how many books are given to people as they come in to a service.
- what other written material is produced and what it looks like.

Summing it up

The differences between people in our local community or congregation can be a real opportunity for learning fresh things about God. Or they can provide a fertile breeding ground for fear, distrust and prejudice. We have described worship as 'bringing my world to God; finding God in my world'. We also need to ask how far there is room for God to introduce us to a world bigger than the one we normally live in. And whether we will thank him for that or not.

Chapter 9

WORSHIP ACROSS THE AGES

'As it was in the beginning, is now and ever shall be: world without end...'

Across the ages?

For almost 2000 years there have been Christians worshipping together – 'at all times and in all places' as the Anglican service puts it. For some people the very idea of being part of a church which spans the ages is a great comfort – especially those who feel only too aware of the shortness of life, and the vastness of eternity. For others it's an excuse for putting that other old Anglican refrain into all too painful practice and keeping things as much the same as possible from year to year.

But as well as spanning the ages of history, most churches also span quite an age-range in their present, and it's that particular age-span that we'll be thinking about in most of this chapter. The needs of, say, an eighty year-old who has been 'born and bred' in a particular church, differ from those of the toddler child of a young couple who have only recently moved into the area. Yet we expect them to worship side by side. Or do we? And in cities the ages are both more and less together than elsewhere. What do I mean?

On the one hand poverty is a great leveller. Cathy is a single mum living with her five children in a two-up/two-down. Her family are thrown a great deal more together than John and Maureen living with their daughter Chrissie in a five-bedroomed detached house with grounds! On the other hand, it may be that children of well-off families learn to talk to adults much more than do children of poorer families. Chrissie is growing up with opportunities for one-to-one relationships with her parents that Cathy's five just aren't likely to get.

In addition, cities frequently have greater proportions of elderly, singles, lone parents, and the inadequate or disadvantaged than elsewhere. These people, too, need to be catered for in our worship. So how can we do this? We shall be looking at the ways in which the idea of the church as family can help, and also at its shortcomings. But we'll begin by considering the pattern of religion 'across the ages' that we have inherited at this point in history.

Giving them religion!

In the not-so-distant past the attitude prevailed that church is for sending children along to, to 'give them some religion'. Both Pauline and Harry are to some degree casualties of that idea – and you can probably think of others like them as well. But to many people that's still what church is about: a place for the very young, the very old and a number of unmarried women who have turned to religion as a consolation for their singleness; all presided over by a sexless and ageing clergyman.

But we need to let it be known that church is for everyone. It's not a 'religious club', or a phase that you grow into or out of, but a family in itself, that all can belong to. Some churches have expressed this by introducing what are known as 'Family Services', where all ages worship together. This ought not to mean a service for traditional families (parents with children) to come together to worship, but a time when the family of the church gathers for worship.

Pauline is in her mid-twenties, single with two children. She'd like to marry the children's father if he were willing, but because he's usually around for the children she feels less hard done by than many others on the estate. Pauline is a private but very caring person who is the first on hand when troubles strike someone else. But she will not come to church. Why? Because when she was younger her parents made her go! And as soon as she was old enough to choose she chose not to go.

Harry is in his forties, and was a child evacuee during the war. The family he was placed with believed in discipline and believed in religion – for the children. They never went to church, but Harry had to go, three times on a Sunday – or his foster father took a belt to him. When he grew up Harry rejected the church and its message with it.

THINK SPOT

1 It has been estimated that 90% of children who attend Sunday School fail to attend church once they are adult. Why do you think this is?

2 Do people in your area see church as 'for the very young, very old and a number of unmarried women'? If you think they do – why is this? If you think they don't – who do they see it as being for?

3 If you have a Family Service, which of the two meanings given above is closest to what you understand by it?

Children in church

It is now becoming a commonplace to note that children are not the church of tomorrow, but part of the church of today. By this it is meant that we are not trying simply to 'baby-sit' for children until they grow up into adults, old enought to understand and take part 'properly' for the first time in worship. Instead we recognise the truth of what Jesus said about children being closer to the kingdom of heaven than adults. And we try to find ways to help them on their own spiritual journey, alongside us as adults. What will that mean for those leading and taking part in worship?

There are some 'basic principles' of worship for and with children in church. These will, of course, need turning into practical ways of doing things, but I don't propose here to tell you how exactly to do that, for two good reasons. The first is that a number of other people have already

Are children important enough to be *given* books?

done that better than I could, and there's little point in duplicating that information here. The second is that a 'formula' for worship that works in one place may be quite inappropriate in another. The people involved, the numbers and balances, vary so much from place to place that it seems better to look at the principles underlying them, and leave you to do the actual applying in your own situation! So here are the principles.

Principles for planning worship for and with children

Do's

- DO learn to understand the differences between children of different ages and how they 'tick' – for example, whereas juniors (7–10s) will love quizzes, infants (5–7s) will probably be happier with simple noisy songs. And pre-schoolers won't relate to activities above their eye-level. You can probably think of your own further examples!
- DO look at what you do through the eyes of a child – do the words of the hymns make sense? Are the books attractive to look at and hold? Are children considered important enough to be *given* their own books?
- DO be prepared for a degree of noise, questions, and disruption as children feel free to be themselves amongst adults – or are noisy babies rushed away into a creche? Would a toddler cause chaos in the sanctuary?
- DO look for ways in which adults can learn from children and children can learn from adults – have you considered organising some activities that all ages can do together? You can spend a very successful hour or so cooking together, for example. More about this below.

Don'ts

- DON'T turn worship into children's entertainment – it's at least worth remembering that the dividing line between worship and entertainment exists, even though it may be thin at times and different people will draw it in different places.

● DON'T ask children to do things you wouldn't do yourself – although some children love acting in front of others, asking one or two to 'sing a song to the grown-ups' at short notice can be terribly unfair!

● DON'T embarass either children or adults with activities or requests which are inappropriate to them – whilst some adults will respond readily to the invitation to 'roar really loud like a lion', or 'join in all the actions', other will find it more than they can stand. Putting pressure on everyone to join in is as unfair as singling out individuals to do things they'd really rather not: both are a gross abuse of the power given by standing at the front.

THINK SPOT

1 When Jesus said of children: 'the Kingdom of heaven belongs to such as these' – what do you think he meant? (See Matthew 19:14)

2 Can you think of your own practical examples of the DO's and DON'Ts listed above?

Who are the children?

The children present in many city churches will come from a variety of backgrounds, and in many cases will bear little resemblance to the quiet, well-behaved 'junior church members' of other areas. My wife is involved in our local playgroup. Recently, on a day off in a more affluent part of the city, we saw children from another playgroup waiting for the bus home from a visit to the park. She couldn't believe her eyes! All the children were sitting quietly on the grass verge and the leaders were chatting peaceably behind them. Fifteen minutes later when we passed back that way they were still there. Our experience is of children who don't sit still even for fifteen seconds. It's not that they won't – they just can't!

· Many children in inner-city churches will have one or more of the following in their background:

● a lone parent – sometimes with a bewildering succession of 'fathers'.

● poverty – so they may be poorly dressed and underfed.

● a lack of relationships with adults – this may be due to lack of interest or to some young, single mother's lack of parenting skills.

● erratic discipline – linked to parenting problems. This means that children can have very limited self-control.

● late hours – playing out on the streets (summer), or sitting up watching videos (winter), often of the sex and violence genre.

● victims of abuse – physical, emotional or sexual.

Of course a list like that can make daunting reading, and not every child will be affected by even one of these. But on the other hand there will be some for whom most, if not all, are true – and it does affect how we make space for such children in the church. What might be expected in other types of area, in terms of behaviour or response, will not be appropriate to expect here. It is easy to lose patience with such children – I know, I've done it, far too often for comfort!

But in many ways such children are more truly seen as the victims of what others have done to them, and deserving of our especial love and care than our anger and condemnation. Jesus' words come to mind here about the seriousness with which God views any who damage the faith of 'one of these little ones', when he said that 'it would be better for that person to have a large millstone tied round his neck and be drowned in the deep sea.' (Matthew 18:6).

From theory to reality

So much for theory. What might this mean in practice? The practicalities are that either children and adults are together for worship or they are apart, and in most churches there is some sort of combination of the two approaches. We shall look at the three situations in turn:

Adults apart

This may be for most or all of some services in some churches, or a comparitively rare occasion in others, confined mainly to Sunday evenings. It may be thought that little need be said here about children in worship – but if our description of the church as family is true, then it needs to be remembered that adults worshipping alone is not, as some tend to see it, 'proper worship' but rather 'imperfect worship'. Deprived of the children our response to God is limited.

Indeed many adults enjoy for their own sake what is often called 'children's worship' and that may well be another reason not to put too much emphasis on taking the children away and running a very different sort of service.

Of course, this isn't to deny that there are real differences between children and adults' response to God. It is simply to point out that 'adult' worship may not necessarily be 'better' worship!

Children apart

'Sunday School' is a name that needs burying but is without a widely accepted replacement. But the activities it covers still need to be there. inner-city children will need activities that are even more child-centred than usual, in recognition of the many problems that may be present in a group. Ideally children will be divided into age groups corresponding to those they are used to at school. In our last Manchester church we used the Church Pastoral Aid Society's 'CYPECS' groups structure, and ran a creche for the under-threes, a pre-school group, and then different groups for children of infant, junior and early secondary age. Those over fifteen are expected to remain with the adult church members when we separate.

Leaders (and two should be a minimum in any group) need to be especially loving and alert to what is going on. In the absence of enough leaders – a common problem – it's probably better to lump age-groups together rather than leave lone leaders struggling for survival.

Children apart should not be just entertained with drawings and games. Nor are they there to be pumped full of religious knowledge. Instead, leaders need to look for ways in which they can embark on a spiritual journey in company with the children, learning from them and helping them to learn from their own experiences of life. Didn't Jesus say that 'unless you change and become like children you will never enter the kingdom of heaven'? So worship *for* children becomes worship *with* children, and they will often praise God with far greater genuine enthusiasm than their elders can muster.

THINK SPOT

In a church with limited accommodation, different age groups are meeting at the same time but there are problems with noise levels. Should:

- the preacher ask the children's leaders to keep them quieter so that the adults can get on with their worship?
- the service leader include in the prayers a special thanksgiving for the happy voices?
- the children's leaders ask the adults to turn the organ down and sing more quietly because it's interfering with their activities?

Children and adults together

This may be a weekly occurrence for a whole service, for a few minutes, or in some churches only a once a month occasion, if that. I would suggest that children and adults should worship together on a regular basis, preferably weekly, even if not for the whole service.

This will mean arranging the liturgy, books and words so that children can participate. In a city context it may well be that this is what enables some of the adults present to participate better. Often a non-reader will cope with short 'children's choruses' whereas a full Wesley hymn leaves them cold.

It will be important also to make children aware that they are full members of the congregation whilst they are present. This may be as little a thing as ensuring that all children who want them are given books as they arrive, or be shown in allowing them to take an appropriate part in the worship, for example in short readings, prayers, or talking about or showing something they have done in their own groups. This will not be as a 'performance', but as leaders of the worship of all.

Many churches are feeling their way towards a whole church family approach, not just to worship but also on other occasions. If premises permit, spending all or part of a day together can be important, either on a Sunday or a weekday evening. Activities that are arranged should allow people to mix across the age-range. Children without good experience of adults, even of parents, can have space to develop good relationships with other adults, and adults with little first-hand experience of children can discover for themselves what all the fuss is about! True worship together will then arise naturally out of true belonging together.

Single in God's family

When considering children we noted that many may come from lone parent families. Single people with children may be unmarried, in between partners, divorced or separated, or widowed. And there are also, of course, single adults without children. For all of these, as for childless couples, worship which puts too much emphasis on 'family' can be painfully unhelpful, if by 'family' is meant an idealised advertising dream picture of 'husband, wife and two children'. Yet in its anxiety to defend marriage and family life at a time when they are indeed under threat from various social trends, the church has often seemed to condemn or exclude those who fail to fit into this pattern.

That is why the idea of the church *as* family can be powerful to include those who are excluded by the idea of the church *for* the family. And worship which brings people together across human family lines is a means of affirming and helping those for whom family life has been a source of sadness or disappointment, or simply not a practical experience.

There are, of course, other pictures of the church besides 'family' that may also be helpful to explore. Alongside the 'family church' idea our church has emphasised the 'pilgrim people' idea – that is, God's people on a journey together. It has powerful roots in the Old Testament pictures of the Exodus and the return from Exile, and is picked up by the writer of Hebrews to describe the New Testament church as well – see, for example Hebrews 12:12 and 13:14. And we can recall the story of the boy Jesus travelling to and from Jerusalem for the Passover in a long column of worshippers, and accidentally getting left behind because everyone thought he was with someone else! The picture of a group of all ages, travelling the same path together and helping one another along the way, has a lot to teach us which may go some way towards removing the problems that too much concentration on 'family' alone can lead to.

The place of the elderly

Talk of all-age worship together leads us on naturally to look at the other end of the age-range, the elderly. In many city areas these may well make up the majority of the congregation. This creates both problems and opportunities. Problems, because it may be that an elderly majority is also a backward-looking majority, and that the church is tied to a glorious past rather than open to its future, glorious or otherwise! Opportunities, because old people are often neglected and undervalued in society today, and the church can rediscover a better way of valuing their wisdom whilst respecting their frailties.

... one lady in her eighties put younger ones to shame!

In my experience, many older city people are not necessarily as conservative as their parents were or their equivalents are in 'comfortable Britain'. They may indeed have special memories of the church or area from times past but, having lived through the violent changes in the cities of the sixties and seventies, may also be more realistic about change in the eighties and nineties.

When we asked our congregation to comment and indeed vote on various changes to our worship, we found it was some of the older ones who wanted us to move on. Many younger people were far more stuck in the mud! I well recall one lady from a former church who only became a Christian in her eighties and who put younger ones to shame by her enthusiasm.

So worship with the elderly in mind needn't necessarily be the same as worship according to traditional patterns – good as that sometimes is in its own right. Far more practically, worship with the elderly in mind needs to ensure it is visible, audible and comfortable. More important than the hymns sung or the service used, is the size of the print, the effectiveness of the PA system (or induction loop), the efficiency of the heating and the construction of the chairs! Not forgetting proper provision for the disabled of all ages as well, beginning with decent access for wheelchairs.

In many cities there will be high proportion of single elderly people who often see few people from week to week, and whose social and physical needs are as great as their spiritual ones. Therefore another possibility favoured by some churches is to organise special 'senior citizens services', which may be combined with a lunch or tea and some other special activities. It is important on such occasions that people of all ages are present and take part in the events, not just as 'helpers' but actually sharing in the events themselves, so the day doesn't become yet another gathering of 'mouldy oldies'! The service itself might use favourite hymns and familiar prayers, possibly some simple drama,

THINK SPOT

1 When do the young and old mix in your congregation? Do they worship together or just alongside each other?

2 Could you organise a special event for the elderly in your congregation or area? List the sort of things that such an event might contain, including the worship.

and a short address maybe based on a psalm or some other passage in the Bible relating to the issues elderly people face. As with children, it is important that it doesn't degenerate into an entertainment but retains the qualities of real worship – that it helps those present to bring their world to God and to find God in their world.

Other pictures of the church

This chapter has been dominated to some extent by the idea of the church as family. This is, of course, only one picture of the church; there are many others, equally biblical and reflecting different aspects of its nature. For some people *any* mention of family can be less than helpful, and we may need to examine the way we think and speak of ourselves to avoid making this the main or only picture we use. For example, we've already thought of the church as a pilgrim people.

Again, there are pictures in the Bible of the church as building, or as holy nation, or as chosen people, to mention just three more. Each has its own things to teach us, and its own limitations. What they do all appear to have in common is the idea that the church is not just a collection of individuals who happen to come together on occasion, but that being a Christian means we actually belong together in far more organic way. A family is more than a collection of related people; a building more than a pile of bricks; a nation more than a group of people living in the same place; and a chosen people greater than the sum of the individual choices. Belonging to the church, especially in a city, reminds us that we are better off together than apart. In the words of the three musketeers: 'United we stand. Divided we fall'.

THINK SPOT

What are the strong points and weaknesses for your church of the pictures of the church mentioned above? Can you think of other biblical pictures that might be particularly helpful to some in your congregation?

Summing it up

In the inner-city, 'my world' will almost certainly include people of all ages and all sorts of family background. If I'm to bring that world to God then I must allow my worship to be affected by the experiences and viewpoints of people of all those different types. And if God is to be found in that world, then there must be space for us to come to him together, and to speak to him together, not as separate groups.

Chapter 10

WORSHIP FOR ALL

'I suspect we have passed the time, at least in Urban Priority Areas, when we can expect good numbers of people out there to be just waiting to be invited to church. Evangelism means outreach – we ask God to "send us *out*".'

Colin Buchanan in *The Heart of Sunday Worship* (Grove Books)

It's 6.30pm and the congregation is mostly assembled. It's made up mostly of older people, with a few younger singles and a newly married couple. All those with children are at home having tea, watching the telly or putting the little ones to bed. The service begins with a stirring hymn and continues in a fairly informal, if predictable, form to the sermon, where the preacher exhorts, implores and appeals to any present who don't yet know the Lord Jesus as personal friend and saviour to put that right tonight. Of course, nobody does. In their minds, they've all done that years ago. And no outsider in their right minds would venture into this service. It's advertised as a 'Gospel Meeting'. An opportunity for sinners to repent. In fact its a weekly liturgy for the saints, to remind them of the way they came into sainthood.

A parody? Probably – although not so many years ago it would have been more widely true than we might like to think. But we have now seen the end of the traditional Sunday evening gospel service, which at its best did indeed succeed in pushing thousands of the semi-churched from half-conviction to conversion. It has been overtaken by changes in our lifestyles. People, by and large, don't come out to church in the evenings unless they're already well committed. And most people don't respond to an evangelist preaching in the context of a traditional church service. Although these trends are true everywhere in Britain, they are even more true in inner cities, where many fear going out at night at all. So does that mean that for those of us living and worshipping in cities, our worship and our evangelism just can't be mixed any more?

In this final chapter we shall be looking at the way worship relates to the wider community in which we are set. This will include not just evangelism, but also some wider concerns such as the way we use the 'big events' of the Christian year (Christmas, Easter, Pentecost – and Harvest Festival!), our contacts with people through 'occasional offices' (baptisms/dedications, weddings and funerals), and our whole attitude to what is often called 'folk religion'.

Evangelism and worship

Let's start with that ill-fated evening 'Gospel Meeting' and the questions it raises. If that sort of evangelism is out, then what, if anything, can take its place? It's beyond the scope of this book to explore in detail evangelism 'beyond the church doors', but does that leave us anything at all to look at under the heading Evangelism and worship? Yes, it does. But it's not what a previous generation might have understood by that.

What those who went before us understood as evangelism and worship tended to be typified by what was called the Evangelistic Service. This meant that an ordinary church service became the occasion for a special sermon, aimed at bringing non-Christians to a point where they were ready to become Christians. Often it would end with an 'appeal' for such people to come to the front, or raise a hand, so they could be 'counselled' afterwards about what they had done. This recipe worked very well in its time, and Dr Billy Graham is still making it work very well on the grand scale. But it's my belief that in the local setting, especially in the city, it's had its day.

The basic problem with this approach was that it assumed people would be willing to come to such a service. And that, in turn, assumed that 'going to church' was a reasonably familiar thing to do for most people – even if it wasn't part of their present everyday life. But for most people nowaday, not only is going to church not part of their life (weddings and funerals apart), but it has become so alien an experience that the very idea of it is hard to comprehend. Those of us who attend week in week out may well fail to realise just how strange our activities seem to the majority of our friends and neighbours; just how unknown what takes place behind those closed doors is to those who have never passed beyond them. So to come to any sort of event in church is a major step in itself. And we certainly cannot assume that an evangelistic service – especially if advertised as such – will draw anybody fresh in at all. It's far more likely to have the opposite effect!

On the other hand, it's my belief that worship needn't be seen in this way as a necessary, but almost accidental, accessory to evangelism. Instead, properly conducted, it can be an evangelistic event in itself. If the church is properly welcoming to strangers; if the service is easily comprehensible and the atmosphere accepting; if the worshippers themselves look as if they are actually joining in with what is going on rather than it simply happening to them – then any open-minded visitor should be able to sense the presence of God, and perhaps be challenged in some way by parts of what they see and hear. Maybe what Paul describes in

Susan

Susan was a sprightly seventy-year old, who often nipped out to collect her elderly neighbour's paper on a Sunday morning. One warm Sunday the church nearby had its doors wide open and she was arrested by the music floating out: 'He's got the whole wide world in his hands'. Interested, she came closer, and seeing her, a young man at the door stepped outside and asked if she would like to come in. 'I think I would,' said Susan, and in she came. Speaking to me later about that service she explained how the whole service left a permanent mark on her, as she heard that Jesus died to forgive our sins. 'It sounded about right to me,' she said. 'A bright person could believe that; a not so intelligent person could grasp it too.' Susan returned the next week, and the next, and very soon reached the fruition of a life-long religious search for peace of mind, as she accepted Jesus into her life.

And all because the doors were open, a sidesperson had been welcoming, and the words of the service had made sense to her!

1 Corinthians 14:24–25 will happen: 'He will be convinced of his sin…and he will bow down and worship God, confessing, "Truly God is here among you!"'

Out in the open?

Another way of combining worship and evangelism is to take the church out to the people. Of course in the British climate this is most safely confined to the summer months, but what is to stop you taking your service outdoors? There are various ways this can be done: in some areas a 'march of witness' may be the best way to let people know the church is alive and well in their midst. If this is your choice, then thought needs to be given to matters such as route, stewarding, banners, music and such-like – not forgetting to inform the police of your plans! In some places this march dimension may be the main focus of such an event. Others may wish to combine it with a short stop or two, in a suitable venue, for a mini-service of songs, prayer, testimony and greeting. The venue needn't even be outdoors – although if it is, a suitable PA system is necessary. But old people's homes, friendly community centres, pubs – all could be the occasion for a 'one-off' export service! In other areas the walk dimension may be a lesser factor and the service a greater. An entire service could then be held outdoors in a suitable spot, with just a minimal procession there and back – or even gathering there to start with. A less adventurous alternative for beginners, if your premises are suitable,

THINK SPOT

1 Think of the last time you attended an 'evangelistic service'? How well do you think it achieved it's aims?

2 How evangelistic is your normal worship? How could it be made more so?

might be simply to move into the church grounds, so passers by can see what you get up to, perhaps even join you. We have tried all these approaches and found them to be of value in our local situation. And the value can be increased ten-fold if you can do it all together with other local churches!

Just a word of warning, however, about such Marches for Jesus as they are also known. There can be a thin dividing line between confidently proclaiming the faith and aggresively intimidating the neighbourhood! Indeed what is seen by the marchers as the first may often be felt by the people as the second! I do not myself believe triumphalism has any part in our Christian witness today. There is what I see as a strong strand of aggressive, militaristic thinking in much modern Christianity, which we need to think carefully about before taking on board. Of course the central truths of Christianity are that in his death and resurrection Jesus has conquered the powers of darkness and won a victory both in time and effective for eternity. In that sense there has been a battle and we are on the winning side. But, on the other hand, if you compare the times the Bible actually calls us 'soldiers of Christ' or invites us to take up arms – especially against fellow human beings! – my judgement is they are considerably outweighed by the times we are exhorted to be gentle, loving, caring and peaceable! Even in the classic passage where Paul speaks of 'the armour of Christ' we see that it is primarily defensive, and aimed at protecting us from Satan, not helping us stick the boot into the world. Generally, whenever military metaphors are used, their overwhelming force is that our 'weapons' are precisely *not* 'of this world' and neither, therefore, should be the spirit in which they are wielded.

THINK SPOT

1 What would be the advantages in your situation of planning worship in the outdoors? What would be the problems?

2 Do you agree with the dangers suggested in Marches of Witness? If so – how would you go about avoiding them?

The warring instinct is strong in many of us and it may be that sometimes, rather than letting it be transformed by the love of Christ, we simply redirect it into what we take to be his service. It ain't necessarily so! So before venturing onto your streets, look carefully at what you plan to do and ask yourself the question: 'If I were a non-Christian watching this event, would it speak to me of the love of God or the self-righteousness of Christians?' You may need to review your plans a little in the light of the answers.

This will be particularly true if your march route takes you into areas where people of other faiths live. Ask yourself how you would feel, for example, about a large contingent of Muslims with banners marching past your home and church, proclaiming their faith in loud slogans. Then try and put yourself in their shoes when we do the same to them. It may be that a gentler approach to proclaiming the faith is necessary in such situations!

Church and community

There are three different 'models' of being a local church which are particularly important to consider in inner-city areas and which affect, amongst other things, the way we worship. Each has its own strengths and weaknesses.

The church as part of the community

This model is particularly strong in some Anglican circles, although not unknown elsewhere. It draws heavily both on what are taken to be the Christian roots of our society, and on the natural sense of religion present in most people. So, for example, the fact that many people who are far from being regular church attenders will still pray regularly at night, or when in trouble (or at least claim to!) is taken as a very positive thing to build upon. Research indicates that many people have had personal and private experiences of God or 'otherness' which they are reluctant to speak of to others; this too is seen as a wonderful starting point. And the fact that the law of the land still gives a privileged position to Christianity in general, and the established church in particular, is also seen as a strength. The church's role, in this model, is to seek out and affirm these 'seeds of faith' in people. If they come to be baptised (or dedicated), married and buried then we are to welcome them with open and uncondemning arms – and if they never darken the church doors again, or avoid the minister for ever after, then that is not necessarily anything to worry about.

Such a church will look for opportunities to build on this sense of natural and civic religion. Harvest festivals, carol services and, to a lesser extent, Easter will be great opportunities for it. If the Scouts want to hold a St George's day parade or the Mayor a civic service, they will look eagerly on it as a fresh opportunity to fill their proper role, as the'conscience' of a still broadly Christian society.

There are some strengths to this model. By taking seriously people's genuine religious experiences it avoids the trap of thinking that God can only be encountered as he is preached or channeled by and through the church – an absurd nonsense apparently believed by all too many Christians! And it is also foolish to act as if there were no such thing as a past Christian tradition which still powerfully affects some things in the present. But weaknesses are also there. In its desire to welcome people where they are at there is a serious danger of failing to challenge them to move on to where God wants them to be! Jesus did welcome the ordinary people – but he also spoke uncompromisingly to them as well as to the rich and powerful about the need to enter into the transforming experience of the kingdom of God. And the gospel from the earliest days has always been a message demanding response, repentance and a new life, not just a comfortable affirming of the old ways.

It is my experience both that 'civic' or 'state' religion is far weaker in the inner-city than it may still be elsewhere, and also that 'natural religion', whilst undoubtedly present, is very far removed from any sensible understanding of the Christian faith. The worship of a church that follows this model too closely will probably be strong on affirmation of both worshippers and what is seen as the good things in the community outside. It may well make those who come feel good, but will be short on challenge, and will cut little ice with those who remain outside.

The church apart from the community

This model of church life is almost the opposite of the first and is correspondingly stronger in the free church and Pentecostal traditions. In it the church is seen very clearly as over against the world. Members join by making their personal commitment to Christ and by implication this cuts them off from those with whom they previously mixed. Life before conversion is generally seen as almost wholly bad, and life outside the church as similarly full of evil and rebellion.

The church's role in this model is to call people to salvation, and escape from the world. It will see the community as a place into which forays may be made, and from which 'captive sinners' are rescued. There will be little interest in the ongoing life of the community for its own sake, for example, local government, tenants or community groups, let alone politics! This will be seen as, at best, 'not the role of the church' and, at worst, as a dangerous diversion from the 'real job' of evangelism. Those showing any interest in religion will be quickly pointed to their own need of salvation, and if they resist taking this journey will either be prayed and harried onto the road, or abandoned as too lost in sin to hear the message.

The strengths of this model are that it does take seriously much biblical material about the nature of humankind, sin and salvation. The emphasis on the wrongness of life without Christ will find ready echoes in the hearts of many for whom city life is just one long procession of disasters and miseries, offset only by temporary moments of pleasure or escape. It does aim to present people with a Christian challenge to their lifestyle and can often be quite succesful on its own terms. Its weaknesses are that it does often limit its understanding of what God is doing simply to the salvation of individual people, to the exclusion of either any realistic attempt at helping them grow as mature people in their faith, or of any understanding that God's concern for justice is expressed within the community at large as well as the lives of individual people. Essentially there is no such thing as 'community' in this model, outside the church.

The worship of a city church operating by this model will be strong on commitment, on challenge to those present, and on prayer against what is seen to be wrong in the world outside. It will not, however, provide any 'easy ways in' to the outsider who will be presented from the word 'Go' with an uncompromising demand to 'submit or be damned'!

The church serving the community

Neither of the above models, again perhaps painted in their cartoon extremes, seems terribly satisfactory, especially when facing the many and deep needs of inner-city communities. The third model, which I personally commend, tries to take the best of the first two and avoid their worst excesses. In it the church is seen as both a messenger and an instrument of salvation. The church is an instrument of salvation in that it takes seriously the command to 'love your neighbour', whether or not that neighbour is about to respond personally to God, and follows the example of Jesus in healing the sick and meeting with the outcast, whether or not they subsequently left all and followed him. But the church is also a messenger of salvation in that it does accept that people do need to hear the challenge of the gospel – both individually and corporately.

In being such a messenger and instrument of salvation, the church can value people for who they are, and their experiences, both religious and otherwise, will be seen as genuine at their own level. To take two personal examples, helping in the battle to get a road crossing installed opposite a school, or challenging a faceless local authority bureaucracy when it attempts to impose its own play-schemes, regardless of the impact on existing users of the community centre, are worthwhile aspects of the church's mission; they affect lives for the better, and are faithful to the teaching Jesus gave that in serving others we serve him. But the individuals caught up in these and other issues still need somewhere along the line to make their own response to the God before whom, one day, they will stand face to face and who will call them to account for their lives.

Two examples

As examples of these models at work I want to take a couple of instances from my own experience of trying to operate on the 'serving the community' model in an Anglican context, and compare it with how I see the other models operating. One examples is from the more individual setting and the other more communal.

1. 'Getting the baby done'

This first example is one that may seem particular to Anglicans, but I believe has its parallels in other Christian traditions. In the first 'part of the community' model, what tends to happen is that this is seen as a chance to welcome someone; so a baptism is arranged, often with little or no attempt to challenge the enquirer with the actual meaning of the service or the significance of the promises they, as parents, will be required to make. This can result in the strange situation of people standing before a congregation (or, as often as not, just before one another) promising to 'turn to Christ', and then leaving, never to be seen again or to show any evidence of turning to Christ in any degree. The community has been served, the religious function of the church has been carried out, but there has been little or no communication and another person has left church convinced that as long as you say the words, 'with your fingers crossed', it doesn't matter what you really believe at all.

In the 'over against the community' model, it is realised that to ask someone from completely outside the church to make promises of Christian commitment without explanation or content is a nonsense. So the enquirers are, gently or otherwise, told that we can't do this unless they have themselves been converted. I have heard that some are encouraged there and then to kneel on the vicarage floor and 'pray a prayer'. More commonly they are expected to turn up regularly at church. Usually, however, they resent this approach and disappear in a huff, to spread the word to all and sundry that 'the Vicar wouldn't "do"our baby.'

The 'church serving the community' model starts from a different point. Whilst not allowing others to tell us what baptism is for or who can and can't appropriately have it, it recognises the genuine feelings which often lie behind the maybe not very articulate request. Time is taken to explain the full meaning of baptism and the promises involved. The parents or, as likely, parent is made to feel welcome from the first contact, through any later visits and eventually in church, if they do decide to come. We use the Anglican service of Thanksgiving for the Birth of a Child as

Michael and Janice

Michael and Janice had been living together for a year or so and their first baby was on the way. Each had a religious background – Michael in a Pentecostal church, Janice as a Roman Catholic – but neither had attended for some years. But they wanted the baby 'done', and so by way of compromise approached me, as their local Anglican minister. Over a few weeks we discussed a lot of things, including their persnal faith and belief, their marital status and services for the coming baby. More to the point, they started to come to church – first Janice, and then Michael. As they came, and as we talked, it started to fall into place. In the event we baptised the baby a week or so before we celebrated their wedding, and the whole family became church members together.

But I am sure it was the impact of worshipping with a believing, lively congregation over several weeks that bridged the gap between my words and the reality of where their lives were at.

THINK SPOT

1 Which of the three types of church mentioned is yours closest to? Do you feel these models are a fair way of looking at churches?

2 How would your church respond to a baptism enquiry from people very much 'on the fringe' of the church? Would you like to change that in any way?

a first means of doing this formally. Then, if parents want to look further into the service of baptism, its full meaning can be explained. It has been my experience that far more 'straight talking' can be done later on if the first experience is of welcome!

2. Carol services

Here we have a typical example of an occasion that is more or less 'expected' of the church at or near Christmas time, but which raises serious questions for many church members and ministers in terms of what exactly we are doing in providing it.

If we take the 'part of the community' model, then a carol service is yet another welcome opportunity of providing a channel for religious feelings. But it risks being simply a 'folk religious festival' which a decreasing number of people in cities want to attend anyway.

In the 'over against the community' model, however, the carol service is either resisted as a distraction from helping the true church celebrate the true meaning of Christmas, or else the presence in church of some people who may be there only once a year is used as an excuse to 'preach the gospel' in a thinly-veiled, evangelistic sermon. This, of course, is open to the accusation of abusing the occasion, and in any case is likely to be resented by those who came for something rather different.

For a number of years the church where I worked had held a traditional Sunday evening 'Carols by Candlelight' and tried various ways of making it meaningful both to regular worshippers and occasional attenders. One problem was that in our particular inner-city area not many people actually *did* want to turn out on a Sunday evening for anything religious, not even a carol service. This was not helped when services moved out of the building and into the nearby community centre – 'Carols by Candlelight' just isn't the same in that sort of setting. So for four years now we have changed tack and organised a Community Carol Service in the centre on a week-night evening. Various community groups are invited to contribute items, but the overall control rests with the church; in this way we have put together services that both channel the local religious feeling that Christmas generates, but still enables us to witness to the Christian difference in our celebrations. It became another 'way in' to the fuller expression of the life of the Christian faithful on Sundays – and of course our pre-Christmas Sunday services are freed to remain a place for the more committed to prepare as we think best. In this way we have tried to be faithful to the model of being a 'church serving the community' in our worship.

Worship for all?

So is there such a thing as 'worship for all'? Only in the sense that the gospel is for all; that the Good News is available to all people, without regard to sex, race, class or any other human category we could come up with. But not, of course, in the sense that everyone is automatically Christian, nor even that all those who hear will automatically respond.

So our worship is to be available to all, regardless of human-made divisions – and, of course, usually it isn't. It must wherever possible meet people where they are, but not where we think they ought to be. And it doesn't aim to leave them there, but to bring them on to a deeper experience of God. For someone who has not yet begun to experience the sort of life that Jesus called 'eternal', this will be where our worship should take them.

Many people outside the church, as much as within it, will at least sometimes feel the need to bring their lives to God. All people outside the church need to bring God into their lives. They fit our definition of worship. Our worship should be for them also – it should be 'worship for all'.

Epilogue

WHERE DO WE GO FROM HERE?

If you used the 'Think Spots' as you used this book, then already you've probably had so many bright ideas about worship in your church that there should be no stopping you. Or will there? It all depends on whether what you think is right for your church is what other people think. So you need to find out.

Why not try out a simple survey on your congregation, or a representative group of them? There's an example in the Appendix. But make sure there's someone who can analyse the answers or it'll be more confusing than helpful!

Then you could get a group together to discuss the sorts of things this book has raised. Maybe even have a Church Thinking Day on worship – invite someone else to come in and think with you, perhaps.

Out of all that you should aim to get some definite ideas of things you'd like to change, or to try out differently. Make sure they're clear ideas, with some idea who should do them. To aim for 'everyone to meet with God more fully week by week' is no doubt very good – but as it doesn't say how this is to be done and is almost impossible to test, as a practical proposition for change it's useless!

These ideas can then be put to the appropriate group in your church and some, at least, should emerge as things to do. They should be tried out for a decent period, and people asked – not all the time, of course! – what they think about it.

But in the end, however you go about it and whatever changes you do – or don't – make, the thing to remember is what it's all about. That we should bring our world to God – and find where God is at work in our world. That may make a rotten motion for the church council. But it's the only test that ultimately matters.

Appendix A

A SIMPLE WORSHIP SURVEY

This is based on a survey carried out within our own congregation, and will need adapting to fit local circumstances.

We used it, after advance notice, in place of a sermon at a morning service, and so got a good response rate. At the same time a simplified version was used with the children's groups, and their replies were put together with those of the adult congregation in the final report to our church council.

It is important to resist the temptation to fill up a survey like this with questions that seem interesting to you at the time, but don't really tell you anything useful or relevant. For example, unless you're particularly interested in seeing if men and women have different views on your worship, there's not much point putting in a question to find out what sex the respondents are.

Similarly 'open-ended' questions should be kept to a minimum, as the amswers are very hard to analyse well. But to include one at the end, as we did, can enable people to get things off their chest that may not otherwise come out.

For advice on how to use this, see the Epilogue!

A General

1 How long have you been worshipping with us?

☐ less than a year?
☐ 1–6 years?
☐ 6–10 years?
☐ over 10 years?

2 What age group are you?

☐ under 21?
☐ 21–30?
☐ 31–40?
☐ 41–65?
☐ 65 plus?

3 What do you think of the following statements?

	Agree	Not sure	Disagree
• It is supremely the minister's job to preach and lead worship	☐	☐	☐
• There should be a group of people in the church to plan and discuss our worship	☐	☐	☐
• Everyone should be given a chance to help plan and lead worship	☐	☐	☐

B Morning services

1 How often do you attend?

- most weeks
- miss a few
- just now and then

2 How do you feel overall about morning services?

- mostly inspiring and helpful
- sometimes helpful, sometimes not
- mostly dull and boring

3 Features of the service.

What is your personal preference on the following things?

	Would like more	About right	Would like less
use of set service book	☐	☐	☐
open worship and praise	☐	☐	☐
traditional hymn	☐	☐	☐
modern songs and choruses	☐	☐	☐

4 Congregational involvement in leading.

What is your view on using more people in leading the following things?

	Would like more	About right	Would like less
preaching	☐	☐	☐
leading the service	☐	☐	☐
leading prayers	☐	☐	☐
reading lessons	☐	☐	☐
giving notices	☐	☐	☐

5 Preaching.

What is your opinion about sermons, on the whole:

	Too little	About right	Too much
length	☐	☐	☐
use of the Bible	☐	☐	☐
practical advice/examples	☐	☐	☐
visual aids	☐	☐	☐

6 Odds and ends

(In our case these were all specific suggestions from an earlier congregational meeting)

	Agree	Unsure/ About right	Disagree
more involvement of children	☐	☐	☐
stop wearing clergy robes	☐	☐	☐
use of 'inclusive language'	☐	☐	☐
start dead on time	☐	☐	☐
taped music before the service	☐	☐	☐
chocolate biscuits at the end	☐	☐	☐

C Sunday evening worship

1 How often do you attend?

- most weeks
- miss a few
- just now and then

2 How do you feel overall about evening services?

- mostly inspiring and helpful
- sometimes helpful, sometimes not
- mostly dull and boring

3 How do you react to the following suggestions?

	Yes	No
should be more different from the mornings	☐	☐
should give a larger role to preaching	☐	☐
should be more room for experiment	☐	☐

D Anything else?

If you have any other comments on our worship, please add them overleaf. Thank you.

Appendix B

RESULTS OF A SURVEY

These figures come from a survey I carried out in Manchester Diocese on behalf of the Worship Committee, in May 1986. In all, replies were received from almost three-quarters of the 109 parishes contacted, which were all those designated as Urban Priority Area at that time.

Amongst other things, both clergy and lay representatives were asked to respond to some statements, drawn largely from *Faith in the City*, by rating them from 1 to 5, as follows:

1 = strongly agree, 2 = on the whole agree, 3 = unsure, 4 = on whole disagree, 5 = strongly disagree.

The statements are ranked below, in order of overall 'average score', which is then given separately for clergy and laity.

In addition the percentage of clergy and laity registering that they 'strongly agree' with each statement is given. This, taken with the average score, indicates the spread of opinion on each statement.

1. Those leading worship should pay special attention to pronunciation and clarity of diction.

	Average score	% strongly agree
All	1.76	
Clergy	2.02	34
Lay	1.44	63

2. It is very important that ordinary members of Urban Priority Area churches are encouraged to participate in leading worship.

	Average score	% strongly agree
All	1.89	
Clergy	1.82	55
Lay	1.98	42

3. Obstacles to comprehension in worship should be due only to the 'otherness of God' rather than the 'otherness of Anglicanism'.

	Average score	% strongly agree
All	1.90	
Clergy	1.79	51
Lay	2.05	30

4. Worship should be conducted with as much thought for the occasional visitor as the regular attender.

	Average score	% strongly agree
All	2.20	
Clergy	2.42	26
Lay	1.92	46

5. The use of religious symbols in Urban Priority Areas is very important.

	Average score	% strongly agree
All	2.21	
Clergy	1.97	46
Lay	2.50	32

6. Anglican forms of worship should be recognisably the same across the Church of England.

	Average score	% strongly agree
All	2.28	
Clergy	2.49	8
Lay	2.02	38

7. The gospel can be proclaimed in Urban Priority Areas as readily through personal testimony as through objective preaching.

	Average score	% strongly agree
All	2.39	
Clergy	2.31	29
Lay	2.48	16

8. The language of worship should be adapted to suit the local culture.

	Average score	% strongly agree
All	2.56	
Clergy	2.29	22
Lay	2.90	8

9. An atmosphere of informality in worship is to be encouraged.

	Average score	% strongly agree
All	2.81	
Clergy	2.50	23
Lay	3.21	8

10. The Urban Priority Area church must 'be prepared to communicate through feeling rather than the mind, through non-verbal communication rather than verbal'.

	Average score	% strongly agree
All	2.82	
Clergy	2.61	18
Lay	3.08	4

11. Existing church buildings form one of the largest obstacles to church life in Urban Priority Areas.

	Average score	% strongly agree
All	2.86	
Clergy	2.90	32
Lay	2.94	14

12. The charismatic movement has proved to be a great blessing to the Church of England.

	Average score	% strongly agree
All	2.92	
Clergy	2.71	16
Lay	3.19	8

13. Present restrictions on authorised forms of service are a stranglehold on more authentic worship in Urban Priority Areas.

	Average score	% strongly agree
All	3.20	
Clergy	3.20	15
Lay	3.21	15

14. The Alternative Service Book as a book is unsuitable for the worship needs of Urban Priority Area parishes.

	Average score	% strongly agree
All	3.34	
Clergy	3.05	19
Lay	3.70	10

15. The practice of worshippers coming and going during a service is not to be discouraged.

	Average score	% strongly agree
All	3.69	
Clergy	3.33	7
Lay	4.14	2